Birding from the Hip

To the readers of Birdwatch magazine and its editor, Dominic Mitchell, for being at the start of all this.

Title: Birding from the Hip
Subtitle: A Sound Approach anthology

Text: Anthony McGeehan

Original music: Simon Emmerson, Richard Evans, Kate Garrett & Barney Morse Brown
Bird sound recordings: Magnus Robb, Arnoud B van den Berg, Mark Constantine & Killian Mullarney
Voice recording producer: Elizabeth Rice
Narration: Anthony McGeehan & Mairead McGeehan

Photographs: Anthony McGeehan with additions from Tom Ennis, René Pop, Bruce Mactavish, Gerald Romanchuk, Aurélien Audevard, Eric Dempsey, Michel Geven, Ken Knowles, Eric Koops, Tom McGeehan, Brian S Patteson, Thierry Quellenec, Franck Renard, Ran Schols, Matthieu Vaslin, Michel Veldt, Gary H Zahm & Tim Zurkowski

Sound editing: Simon Emmerson & Magnus Robb
Photo editing and lithography: René Pop
Content editing: Mark Constantine
Text editing: Arnoud B van den Berg
Graphic designers: Anneke Boekhoudt, Cecilia Bosman & Mientje Petrus

The Sound Approach: Arnoud B van den Berg, Mark Constantine & Magnus Robb

© text, design and sounds: The Sound Approach
© artwork: Killian Mullarney
© photographs: the photographers as indicated

Published by The Sound Approach, 29 High Street, Poole, Dorset BH12 1AB, UK © 2009
Printed by Tienkamp en Verheij, Groningen, Netherlands

ISBN: 978-90-810933-3-0
NUR-code: 435

Cover and CD labels: Northern Lapwing and Common Ringed Plover (*Killian Mullarney*)

You can order this book by phone: +44(0)1202-676622 or online: www.soundapproach.co.uk.

Birding from the Hip

A Sound Approach anthology

ANTHONY MCGEEHAN & THE SOUND APPROACH

Contents

Acknowledgements

When I first heard, back in 1990, that I would be on a four-man birding trip to New Jersey with a guy who was a perfumer, I had misgivings. I even began to wonder why I had been invited along. It turned out that Mark Constantine had plans for me. Coming from Ireland, my virginal skin had never been ravaged by a mosquito. Saint Patrick had swatted the lot. Constantine was developing a potion that protected the 'wearer' from mosquitoes and to test it, he took me to Great Dismal Swamp in Virginia. The place was hot, steamy and humid. We were also after Swainson's Warblers, which were probably there, if only we had been able to focus binoculars through the seething smog of insects. He smeared me from head-to-toe with the experimental *Bug-geroff* cream. It smelled a little like honey and turned me into a walking termite mound. Its inventor walked past me but only so the ten mosquitoes that were bothering him would join their heptabillion mates dining on me. *Bug-geroff* was sold to the US military after that. Apparently, it is holding the line against the northward advance of Killer Bees in southern California. Almost twenty years later, Mark came up with another plan. He asked me to write this book. Among its pages are many stories that, but for him, would never have happened. So I am blessed. The last twenty years would not have been the same without him.

A cover can make or break a book's appeal. I love the cover artwork that Killian Mullarney conceived and painted. Down the years, he has been a great supporter of *Birding from the Hip*. A Dutch women team came up with the book's design.

'The Golden Girls' are Cecilia Bosman, Anneke Boekhoudt and Mientje Petrus. Under their feminine gaze the contents were given a style makeover and numerous questions – some of them personal – led to fresh admissions: "Is that your real hair? Does Mrs McGeehan know any lawyers?" I owe a lot to Holland. Shrugging off the difficulties of working below sea level, René Pop was magnificent as photographic tsar. On a par with his indefatigable editorship of *Dutch Birding*, Arnoud B van den Berg not only scrutinized the text but also managed, along with Cecilia Bosman, to pull off the miracle of creating a book out of several hundred emails.

Back in Ireland, Ken Douglas was a master craftsman in use of English over many years and drummed grammar into me (or should that be 'Ken drummed my grammar?'). Many friends helped in a host of ways. Gerry Carr retyped original versions of old columns and then discussed content with me over several intense, *Birding from the Hic!* liquid editorials. John Scovell provided numerous bright ideas, laughs and several inspired illustrations. DIM Wallace and Eric Dempsey were both fantastic conduits in encouraging me to keep going. Thanks also to Shaun Robson and Nick Hopper who, at the eleventh hour, checked the text for typos to secure a free cosy. Every photographer that I contacted for images bent over backwards to help. I would especially like to thank, from North America, Bruce Mactavish, Ken Knowles, Brian S Patteson, Gerald Romanchuk, Gary R Zahm and Tim Zurowski; from the Low Countries, Arnoud B van den Berg, Michel Geven, Eric Koops, René Pop, Franck Reynard,

Chris van Rijswijk, Ran Schols, Michel Veldt, Edwin Winkel and Pim Wolf; from France, Aurélien Audevard, Matthieu Vaslin and Thierry Quelennec; from Ireland, Eric Dempsey and Tom Ennis. In Spain, Ricard Gutiérrez was a consummate fixer for trips within Catalonia and despite it being a 'foreign country', adjoining parts of northern Spain. Elizabeth Rice was the saint who produced the readings on the CDs and tidied up all the written material so it read more easily. She is a French-polisher of English. At *The Sound Approach* headquarters in deepest Dorset, Matt Fairhall organized logistics and kept everything legal – or I hope he did.

Magnus Robb played a major and incalculable role. He made the beautiful brand new bird sound recordings that Mark Constantine asked me to select for the book. This involved much planning and many chilly hours in the field both by day and at night. Watching him at work was a delight. Along with Pim Wolf, the pair of us shared an amazing winter trip to Spain to record Cranes and Dupont's Larks. Then it was Ireland's turn. Trying to find quiet locations for recordings was extremely difficult. We were saved by freak serene and blissful weather in mid-March and scrambled to catch a boat to Tory Island off the coast of Donegal to record Lapwings, Skylarks and Rock Pipits. There, the island's king extended his patronage to our endeavours. Magnus, whose Edinburgh manners and politeness are always evident and an asset, was amazed. Coyly, he asked me if it was permissible to ask the king a question - could he even do such a thing? Was there a protocol that had to be followed? Should he curtsy before asking, submitting, or giving the king a question?

Furthermore, should the royal personage be addressed as 'One'? I told him that, whatever he said, to be careful not to start with the line, "Your majesty, is it all right to give One, one?" In the end we bought the old boy a pint and he told us that we could walk wherever we liked. Thanks, your Highness!

When the readings for the two CDs were completed they were as naked as the cries from a new-born baby. Simon Emmerson swaddled them with soothing melodies and has lulled the narrators into believing that perhaps Belfast accents are not so bad.

And finally, here it is, the most fought-over dedication in the history of post-William Caxton typesetting. Who will get the nod? Well, it is to you all. This book is dedicated to Tony, Maureen, Mena, Mary (Will you look at him - he is the spitting image of his identical twin!), Gerard, Kathryn, Tom and, especially, Mairead.

Birding from the Hip - a second coming

Phrases are funny things. The best and most perceptive are ancient and anonymous, which makes you think that there really is nothing new under the sun. 'Cometh the hour, cometh the man,' seemed to ring true for me when I read about the launch of *Birdwatch* by Dominic Mitchell back in 1989. I sensed youth, energy and a journalistic flair. At last, I said to myself, someone is going to cast off the tweeds and give birds a new appeal. If the magazine was going to make a difference it had to survive, which meant attracting subscribers. I coughed up right away but I also did something that I had never done before. I wrote to the editor – to wish the venture success. I did not expect a reply but I got one anyway. To broaden the publication's interest, Dominic wanted to add a bit of Irish flavour, in particular an article about the best autumn hotspots. British readers would find that really interesting, he said. Well yes, too darned right they would – and I would be guilty of giving away national silverware and destined to be remembered as a Celtic Judas Iscariot. Still, I didn't want to let him down, so I penned a site guide to Rockall with a seawatching supplement directing folk to Lough Neagh. Duty done. Or so I thought. He was back for more. He was looking for columnists. I resisted. For one thing, I remained fearful of reprisals following my first foray into print. Eventually, we agreed a formula. Since the magazine was bimonthly, I would only have to write six articles as a kind of trial. What should I write about? Dominic didn't know what he wanted. Rather, he knew what he didn't want. Safe was out, conventional was out, Blue Tits were out, as was anything that smacked of 'Oh, silly me, birdwatching's only a hobby.' "Yeah baby," I replied. We decided that a title was

needed. I said, "Well, I better pick something that purports to be potentially libellous in case we wind up in court and then, in the magazine's defence, you can argue that you were only being provocative to defend the liberty of the birding press." "I hope I am not going to regret this," he said. With that, the phrase 'Shooting from the hip,' was dusted down, modified, and given a quill.

I cannot remember what the first column was supposed to be about. The subject was abandoned when Killian Mullarney found Ireland's first Western Sandpiper. I dashed off to see the rarity and decided that I'd try my hand at doing a kind of Alistair Cooke-turned-embedded-twitcher report. I discovered that the effort of writing didn't bring any satisfaction. The sense of embarrassment was so acute that for months I couldn't bear to look at the published text. I wished that I had never started – or at least that Dominic had misspelled my name. When I was still in short trousers and received a school prize for a nature study diary, I got my picture taken. I was captioned in the local rag as Ann McGahan, which saved my bacon. People asked if it was really me that received the prize. Like Saint Peter, I was able to deny the story three times: I was not a typing error, I would never write namby-pamby stuff about birds and I didn't have legs like a girl (I never wore short trousers again). If the *Birdwatch* excursion was going to last, I decided that preparation was key. I drafted a list of topics and tried to settle into a routine. Sometimes a good title would launch me, or a line that had a pivotal quality – a peg upon which I could hang a thousand words. Then the worst happened.

The magazine went monthly. I panicked. I could never come up with fresh true-to-life material every four weeks. It felt as if, for a bet to amuse my mates, I had performed a one-off streak only to find that they ran off with my clothes and left me permanently exposed. Then, I cracked it. I watched *Marathon Man*, starring Dustin Hoffman and Laurence Olivier. For authenticity, Hoffman took up marathon running to help play his role. If his lines were to be delivered through a breathless sweat after hours pounding the track, then so be it – he would be that tortured athlete. Olivier got fed up with all the waiting; it was exasperating. Interviewed after the film, he said that he gave Hoffman a bit of advice that led to a breakthrough in filming. He had told him to forget the running and try acting instead. I did the same. I decided that, if I wrote tales about birdwatching, facts would not be allowed to stand in the way of a good story.

After several years I quit. For no real reason, although I detected early signs of grumpyhood, I felt it was best to go. Subsequently, friends at *Dutch Birding* persuaded me to contribute some light reading to the journal. Since their national birding ethics are almost Utopian – all for one and nobody gets paid, like free love minus the love – I was flattered to be asked. I wrote *Totaal Vogelen* (Total Birding) for three years until the considerable strain of writing in a foreign language wore me out. Sometimes I bumped into *Birdwatch* readers who wondered what happened to me. I just got older. "No," they were kind enough to continue, "whatever happened to that stuff you wrote?" The truth was that it was lying around in old magazines, the equivalent of so many discarded coke tins kicking around a Belfast street.

You don't have to get too close to me to know that cosmetics are not my forte. They are, however, Mark Constantine's stock-in-trade although not his lifeblood, which is bird sound. When my mother found out that he had persuaded me to write this book she said, with that unerring insight that is the prerogative of mothers, "I knew that you would listen to him in the end, he makes lovely soap." I have been a reluctant writer. Slower than the pace of evolution and easily distracted. It was not honeyed words or faint praise that got me going. It was a good telling off, wagging finger and all. I could surrender to negativity, apathy and a loss of enthusiasm. Fine. But if I went bad would I want it said that I never did anything good? I could finish up sounding like Marlon Brando in *On the Waterfront*, a failing boxer reminiscing about a road not taken: "You don't understand. I coulda had class. I coulda been a contender."

A long time ago I stumbled across illustrations of birds on cards that came free with packets of PG Tips tea. Shortly after, I graduated to a battered copy of *The Observers Book of Birds*. Both were from my dad who got the cards from a lorry driver and the book from a pigeon-fancier. Each was handed over 'for the wee lad.' And so I became a birdwatcher. The strange thing was, the birds existed not in life but in my mind's eye. I can still remember clapping eyes on my first Starling. It was exhilarating to see the real thing. The Book of Revelations had come to life. From that point on I was embarked on a treasure hunt. It became an addiction since the supply of species was inexhaustible. Furthermore, the harder I tried, the greater was the reward.

Why do I like birds? They are beautiful and live fascinating lives, but there is something else. They are free and we are not. They survive on their wits and go wherever they need to go. Chicks are born programmed to fly to the ends of the Earth. Their journey may be tough but it is a 'good hurt' if they perish on the way.

Our inheritance is passports and the Health and Safety at Work Act (1974). *Birding from the Hip* was never about such humdrum. Who reads tedium? Look upon the stories as stepping-stones I used to keep my feet dry and not sink into life's mire. I hope you enjoy them, although I worry that you might not: which is why they are in a book whose dimensions double as a draft-excluder fitting most back doors. Surveying them all, arranged neatly like a class of expectant P1s assembled for their first day at school, makes me feel edgy. I know they are trying to look their best and are under orders to behave. However, chaos is bound to ensue, leaving you, dear reader, heading for the back cover and eBay. If so, I apologise. They were never meant to be the funniest stories ever written, they just happened to me while in the company of birds. As John Lennon replied when asked by a sycophantic reporter if he considered Ringo Starr to be the greatest drummer in the world: "Eh? In the world? Why he isn't even the greatest drummer in The Beatles."

Boy meets **rail**

You cannot change the past and my memories of it are wallpapered with birds. Those were the days before moult was invented. Plumages were set for life. All species wore breeding dress perpetually and there were no such things as juveniles, let alone first-calendar-years. There were just two age categories – adults and chicks. Furthermore, bats counted as birds. And why not – they had wings, didn't they?

Summers were long and winters were spent indoors reading *The Observer's Book of Birds*. In our house, apart from the rent book, there wasn't anything else to read. Half the pictures were in black-and-white, which proved to be an identification pitfall until, on the cusp of my teens, I worked out what the words 'depicted in monochrome' really meant. So, in life, Siskins were actually green and yellow – and not shades of Pied Wagtail grey.

Nevertheless, as a means of putting names to faces, the little brown book was brain food with the target-spotting potency of an al-Qaeda training manual. Not surprisingly, it sparked my first ambition. I yearned for a pair of Wellingtons since, not knowing any other birdwatchers, I didn't miss binoculars. I remember my father taking me to a pawn shop to look at a pair and when the man behind the counter said they cost "Two pounds, ten shillings and sixpence," dad nearly had a heart attack. I didn't

like them anyway – actually they were opera glasses – and the bloke was creepy; he had bad breath and bony fingers like a dentist.

Instead, I desperately wanted a pair of wellies. With my one pair of shoes I wasn't allowed to walk across wet fields after Common Snipe or go anywhere near the tickertape clouds of shorebirds on Belfast Lough. Tramping through marshes or across mudflats would have resulted in me being put up for adoption.

Getting close views was the next challenge. For that I needed 'spyglasses'. Around our way, if you used big words such as binoculars, you ran the risk of being thumped for being a show-off. Forget seeing birds in the garden. We did have a garden, but bird tables and strings of peanuts were unknown in Ireland. The BBC patented them a few years later in an episode of *Blue Peter*. Sneaking up to a nest with a terrified Blackbird or Swallow incubating at arm's length was a good way to see details of adults – and then eggs.

Singing birds required different tactics. Sedge Warblers tended to perch where you could see them, thereby avoiding the necessity of hurling rocks into vegetation to startle the songster into view. On the other hand, unobtrusive Grasshopper Warblers were mortared. However, one species remained steadfastly

You can see the problem – even a leprechaun wearing lederhosen would struggle to track down a Corncrake in this habitat.

invisible for years. Corncrakes were a summer soundtrack playing in every pasture tall enough for the species to hide in. The phantom became my nemesis. At nine I ran after the sound in short trousers, by ten I was in jeans and could charge through nettles but at eleven I still hadn't seen one. Short of napalm, I was bereft of ideas.

The goddamn bird even got me into trouble. I was playing outside-right for the school soccer team and could hear a Corncrake calling from meadows at the side of the pitch. It sounded close, closer than the opposing team's outside-left. In fact, he was closer and streaked past to score. My teacher was furious when I told him that I had been distracted by a Corncrake – or 'Landrail' (alas I got no reprieve for erudition in supplying the species' alternative name). Perhaps the games master sensed that I was torn between soccer and birds. He needn't have worried; I decided to combine the two.

It happened like this. I persuaded the rest of the forward line to help me nail a Corncrake. The nearest craking male to home was in the grounds of a local Presbyterian church. On a scale of fire and brimstone, trespassing there would risk punishment of fizzing white-hot intensity. However, the draw was irresistible. The walls that bounded the site effectively isolated the quarry. If we rushed forwards at once, surely the bird would reveal itself? I was so confident of success that I borrowed a pair of spyglasses for the hunt. They belonged to old Jimmy McGreechan, an aged bird fancier who trapped Bullfinches and other wild birds that I drooled over in his aviary. The optics he lent me had German writing all over them – just the gear for the mission.

It felt like a mortal sin when I climbed over a Protestant church gate. The varnished wood, neatly trimmed lawns and weedless gravel pathways all seemed to be watching. Quickly and silently, we stepped into the jungle at the rear of the oratory. As I know now, the Corncrake was using the church walls as an amplifier to throw its voice. At the time, the rasping echo had a banshee creepiness about it. We acted fast. When it paused to draw breath I signalled to the troops who took off like a stampede. The platoon halted at the sound's epicentre, birdless. We tried again. Resolve weakened. Better to scarper rather than wait for the police, who we imagined were probably on their way. Panic gripped big Joe Monaghan. I knew he would be the first to chicken out. He claimed that he heard a voice in the church and legged it.

Well, that did the trick. He got an even bigger fright when a bird with bright ginger wings exploded at his feet. I could see it perfectly. It was wondrous. The pink bill shone like mother-of-pearl on a face of lapis lazuli blue. It was the embodiment of everything a mythical bird should be.

I was changed after that, and became indelibly connected to the wildlife of this planet. I don't know whether I underwent a biblical 'road to Damascus' conversion, or if the Corncrake was Eve, my forbidden fruit in a Garden of Eden. Either way, the operation's de-brief established that life, with birds in it, certainly tasted sweeter. Birdwatching had become my religion, thank God.

January 2005
Birdwatch

Another view from the Hubble Telescope.

Great Northern
Diva

A question. *The* question. Magnus asked it out of the blue. But I couldn't answer it. I had to think. A forgotten memory had been awakened. I spoke but I didn't hear the words. I was rewinding to a childhood world. What was the question?

"What bird sound did you hear first?" Cuckoo clocks didn't count, nor did bath ducks. A coo from a real pigeon would count, as would a crow's caw. Depending on the time of the year, screaming Swifts might have been in the skies over my pram in the garden – or a winter Robin singing underneath streetlamps on my way to school? Whatever that John Hancock species was, I could only nominate it if I could identify it. Well, I was able to identify it. The process took half a century to reach a conclusion, however.

Most people, when told that the first bird recognized on call by a four-year-old boy was a Great Northern Diver, would be astonished or disbelieving – unless the child was born into an Eskimo family who lived beside tundra lakes. Magnus, who possibly was born to Eskimo parents, immediately wanted to know which part of the diver's repertoire I had heard. Was it the yodel, tremolo, or wail? I had to come clean. I might have misidentified a Peacock. I cited mitigating circumstances – I had

no binoculars and may have been confined in a high chair and sucking on a bottle of Ribena at the time. The reason the call left such a vivid and lasting impression was because – I don't quite know how to say this - it gave me nightmares. Magnus was intrigued, so I told him the story.

Pacifying children has been a problem for mothers since the days of Cain and Abel. With the invention of children's television in the early 1960s, things got a lot easier. That's when I came along. The BBC was clearly in on the plot to shut up the nation's children, since broadcasts were timed to coincide with a late morning dip in maternal sugar levels and went under the propaganda banner of 'Watch with Mother'. I guess that was how my mum came to notice her son's leanings favouring the natural world over humans. Apparently, I used to throw my rattle at the screen when *Andy Pandy* appeared but was entranced when *Tales of the Riverbank* commenced. I took the dummy out of my mouth and sat there like a stone cherub for each tale of mishap and adventure involving Hammy Hamster, Roderick Rat and their band of furry and feathered friends.

Outdoors in the adult world, things were not going well – the Cuban missile crisis was one massive worry about which I was oblivious. Little did I know it, but I too was about to get my first taste of anxiety. Instead of its usual daytime setting, one episode of *Tales of the Riverbank* began at dusk. Johnny Morris, the storyteller who normally spoke in friendly animal voices, invoked hushed tones to create a mysterious black night. The dimly lit monochrome images told a tale of ducklings absconding from their mother and illicitly observing the moon coming to Earth. The combination of trembling baby ducks and low-voiced narration was spooky, yet it was something else that put the fear of God into me. It was an eerie, faraway sound that blew in from the darkness. It was neither a shriek nor a grotesque whine but it had a similar effect. Its utterance ushered in a sense of coldness and dread. I did not know what it was, but the sound stuck.

Blessed with a perfect voice for the job, I wonder how much a Great Northern Diver would charge to haunt a house?

Years later I worked it out, or thought I did. I heard a recording of Great Northern Diver and something snapped, big time. Could that have been my terrifying sound of toddlerhood? It certainly seemed similar. Doubt flooded in. Why among all the quacks and snuffles of riverbank wildlife would there be a wailing Great Northern Diver – especially at night? Probably, the dubbed sound was an owl. I explained this to Magnus and only then I came to realise that I wasn't happy. After all this time it would be nice to know the truth.

Might the original programme tape still exist? Surely the BBC would maintain a film archive? I asked friends, like me, all 1960s baby-boomers. Most of them remembered the series, although no one knew how the footage might be traced. A kind elderly lady at BBC Broadcasting House did her best but failed to locate anyone that might assist with my enquiry. She did, however, say something significant. She wondered if I had asked a child to help. "They are much smarter than us, you know." So I asked my son. He googled the title, ebayed a videocassette, and clicked on my credit card details (I didn't know he had them). Volume one of *Tales of the Riverbank* hit the hall carpet 48 hours later.

It was the best £5 I ever spent. Sound unlocks memory far more deeply than pictures. I had no idea what I was in for when I hit 'play'. What happened next was like plonking myself down in a physiatrist's chair. In just 35 seconds I went from title music to Johnny Morris's first sentence: "The riverbank is a very active place on a summer's afternoon, but just as interesting things happen at night," and then – BAM! – a Great Northern Diver cry filled the background. It was a fairytale ending. Except, there was more. The story was exquisitely written. When I first heard it I would not have understood the words. I hung on

them now; they were a rare tapestry, a treasure unearthed: "And then Roderick Rat tells Hammy Hamster the story of the night the moon came down to bathe. The moon was a great gleaming ball of orange tossed up against the inky black sky. Shafts of moonlight drifted over the tops of the reeds, gilded the still surface of the dark river and painted in shining gold the rustling reeds along its bank. There was no sound except the soft whisper of the river and the croaking of the frogs. How strange the familiar sights of daylight looked by the haunting light of the moon. It is all rather frightening for the ducklings." No wonder I nearly swallowed my dummy. I still sleep with the light on.

April 2008

Gallocanta

It all began back in 1969. I was just out of short trousers but already old enough to know that the world was not in great shape. Forget talk of mutually assured destruction of mankind by nuclear warfare, I was much more worried about habitat loss and threats to big birds. Remember, I was a small boy so the only species that really mattered were birds of prey and albatrosses. Everything else was too wee to impress. At that age fairytales were expected to come true as were heroic actions securing noble victories. Maybe it was a post-war impulse to spread enlightenment and make things better, a reaction to the notion that civilization had been brought to the brink of ruin, but it seemed incumbent on the great and the good to do something and call a halt to the trashing of natural resources. 'Conservation has come of age,' was one headline that I recall. 1970 was designated European Year of Conservation. Twenty-one countries were to meet and agree strategies. More importantly, a wildlife programme was to be screened on television to mark the event. I could not wait to see it. Some rich folk had colour televisions but I didn't know any of them well enough to ask for an invite on the Sunday night that the programme was to be broadcast. My mother suggested that I approached our local priest. I wondered why. I knew that she believed in the power of prayer. Could, perhaps, a dash of holy water empower our tiny black-and-white set to receive a colour picture? Her answer was more pragmatic. The priest had a colour set and she could fix it

for me to watch the programme in the parochial house. Fearing altar-boyhood as the price, I watched at home.

The content was somewhere between gloomy and sobering. At least there was no presenter sashaying in front of the camera, feigning excitement and jabbering hyperbole. What stuck was not the conservation message but the opening sequence. Stack upon stack of migrating Cranes circled slowly against the skyline of a European city. There were chimney pots, television aerials, cluttered rooftops and, I think, minarets. It was probably Istanbul, although in my childhood mind I hoped that it might be some place closer to home – Dublin maybe? The layers of birds rotated gracefully, each in a vortex. Their spiralling reminded me of an LP record spinning slowly on a turntable. The silhouettes were hard black set in a sea of silver light. Colour was superfluous. For the first time I saw what a living Crane looked like. They did not flap or fly sunken-necked like old gentlemen Grey Herons. Cranes, I now realised, were regal. But there was something else. A stirring Spanish guitar riff – Rodrigo's Concerto de Aranjuez – drenched the images with an air of bravura. I was left cheering the birds. Not for long would the city with its traffic noise and pall of pollution impose itself. The lives of Cranes beat to a different drum. Soon the birds would pass onwards to faraway wild places that, if I wanted to locate them, would require use of the school atlas.

Gallocanta. Don't you just want to be there?

A whole new millennium later, I escaped Christmas by catching a cheap flight to Barcelona and going off in search of Pyrenean birds with my son Tom and friend John. The pair had snatched victory from the jaws of defeat several times, including stumbling into a Snowfinch (a personal jinx spanning two millennia) that fed at their feet for the full ten minutes when I was nowhere to be seen. However, everybody's luck ran out on New Year's Eve. Despite being advised against driving to our desired destination – a high plateau lake likely to be frozen solid - we set off for a rendezvous of the 'Ten Things I Must Do Before I Die' variety. El Dorado was Gallocanta lagoon and the attraction was Cranes. The drive became too much for us to complete and we wound up in a one-horse town whose inhabitants were about to celebrate New Year's Eve by going to bed early and turning out the lights. We negotiated beds for the night, tucked away at the end of a dim, echoing corridor at the head of six flights of stairs in a deserted taverna. We were the only guests. John, whose cosmopolitan interests meant that he frequently narrated snippets from his Rough Guide to Spain, clammed up when I asked him to translate the inn's name – Alberge del Bates – into English. In an attempt to get some food, my opening remark to the innkeeper – "Señor, is it possible to eat?" was a flop, despite the first word being in Spanish. I tried again. I spoke more slowly and added stress and extra syllables to the words to clarify them: "Ease it-tah poss-eeble to eat-ah?" Success! The guy motioned us towards a solitary table and we all nodded in unison while mimicking the act of putting food in our mouths. Almost there. The table – I pointed, "tay-bah-lah" – was rickety. Switching to semaphore, I did a passable Magnus Pike impression and gesticulated the message: 'Table wonky, please bring food to room.' More empathetic bowing followed and we stalked off to our garret. Sustenance, great baking-hot

baguettes stuffed with grilled pork and juicy peppers, arrived close to the stroke of midnight and were excellent. John said, "What a superb last supper of 2005." Several minutes later those words seemed apocryphal.

It began as a clanging sound, suggesting a dropped tray in the kitchen. The initial report died out but soon other bangs and thuds grew slowly in loudness. No one spoke. Chewing was suspended. Whatever it was, it was getting closer. Silence. A change came upon the room and Tom held my hand. Suddenly the door handle turned, as though wrenched by a poltergeist. The door was flung open and there, heavily perspiring and wiping sweat onto a lumberjack shirt stood the innkeeper, his face contorted and wild-eyed. It was a scene redolent of Sam Peckinpah. In reality, I had overplayed Magnus Pike. The poor man had assumed that we wanted to eat at the rickety table *in the room*. He had dragged it all the way up the stairs from the bar. Worse was to come. The table was too large to go through the door, despite three people manhandling it. Heaven knows we tried. It was too late to backtrack and try and explain the misunderstanding. Suddenly the innkeeper made a sharp sound as though startled. He directed us to stand guard beside the table. He trotted off at speed but indicated, Lone Ranger style, that we should stay put and await his return. Minutes later he was back, his face beaming. He had something in his hand. It seemed too small to be a saw with which to cut the table in half. In fact it was a key. It opened a larger door to another room and there, seated at the table at some time in the early hours of 1 January 2006, we finished cold baguettes and got some sleep.

If you were Captain Oates camped in a blizzard on the shores of Gallocanta lagoon and were 'going outside and may be some time,' you would only be able to walk on the level for a couple of hours before encountering the hills that encircle the plateau. The lagoon is shallow and the land about it is prairie. Swathes of natural grassland hug the foothills but for the most part the flat land is farmed for grain. The ploughed earth is bright terracotta and five tiny villages along the only road sport pastel colours reminiscent of the Grand Canyon. When you stumble onto a place like this you start to flex your imagination. The light was sharp and the air had a glacial quality. There were no imprisoning walls or fences; the landscape was untamed and sparkled in the late afternoon winter sunshine. It was like stepping into an Ansel Adams photograph. And there, dotted over distant fields or arranged in single file along the lagoon's shoreline, were the Cranes, dozens of them. We got high at the sight of majestic birds in a setting that, for once, did not require the use of an airbrush to blot out human intrusion.

Gallocanta is not just land – it is land and sky. Time chimes slowly, measured by the gentle tolling of church bells. Rising from the plains of Aragón and the valleys of Guadalajara, the rim of the plateau frames the heavens above, rather than permitting a view to a distant horizon. Upper atmosphere winds interweave tributaries of cloud and streak them high overhead, like ribbons at a wedding. In late afternoon the sinking sun suffuses the firmament amber in the west and deep cobalt in the east. As the sun sets, undersides of passing clouds are reddened to pink and then violet. Nothing could be more fitting as a canvas for the arrival of not dozens, but thousands of Cranes. We picked a spot looking south and waited. We were dead quiet and wanted to see, hear and smell everything and remember it forever: the whiff of wood smoke, the glimmer of the first star, the hovering descent of a Marsh Harrier dropping to roost among reeds. Not

everyone could see the first dotted line. It was very thin and slight like a strand of spider's muslin. Then, at certain angles of the light, it was obvious that the shape had an axis many metres wide. On it came, rising like a great wave on the prairie and enveloping us with sound. Throaty bugling rang out above a babble of yelping voices, each competing to be heard above its nearest neighbour. Shrill whistles made by youngsters flying wingtip close to parents were interspersed in the baritone chorus. Last of all came the percussive wind from enormous wings that, we agreed, was felt as much as heard. Once the sun vanished, the rate of passage quickened and the din increased. It was as though the birds were afraid of the dark. It was an unforgettable hour, blazed with triumphant reds and oranges that yielded to moonlight.

Attempting to revisit a happy experience is like waking up from a nice dream and hoping that, if you quickly shut your eyes and bury your head under the pillow, you might get back to where you were in the Land of Nod. However, the only part of the dream that Magnus Robb, Pim Wolf and I wanted to capture in early February 2008 was the soundtrack. Surely, with a count of 12,437 Cranes just days before our visit, we could not go wrong? Aspiring to acquire quality sound recordings is on a par with putting an empty speech balloon over George W Bush's head and expecting him to fill it with words of wisdom. Well, maybe not quite that difficult. Nonetheless, even after two days in the company of several thousand Cranes we had little to show for our efforts. Leads had malfunctioned and a lone tractor ploughed steadfastly beside a key roost site right up to dark. The machine's noise threatened disaster. Dusk was settling and Cranes were starting to arrive. Would the farmer quit for the day? No, he simply turned on headlights and continued.

Cranes: such great birds, and so graceful.

Time was running out. When I mentioned that we ought to get up well before dawn in five below zero and hide among frozen corn stalks, wait for the sunrise and hope that the morning's flight might pass close overhead, Magnus paused for a long thoughtful moment, as John Wayne might have done, and said,

"Men, it will be okay." I overheard Pim say "One heck of a plan," in a quavery voice. He fell silent and took deep drags on his cigarette after that. The sky was clear when we lay in ambush. There was no moon, so we had the benefit of maximum darkness. The night, however, was far from black. We lay on our backs and looked at the stars. Lying down and gazing upwards rids you of the feeling that the sky is a canopy. Gazing into space made me think of Napoleon, Julius Caesar, Galileo and other giants, now long dead, who saw the same view of Ursa Major that I beheld. No one spoke, and for a good reason. The twin microphones, despite being placed nearly a hundred metres away, were so sensitive that even the sound of unzipping a jacket would register. Not that anyone would unzip anything in such cold. We kept as still as Lot's wife. I began to see the faint tracery of frosted branches in the trees to my left and could hear stirrings from Crane legions less than a kilometre away. To the east, over my shoulder, the sky had suddenly grown imperceptibly lighter. That did it. The Cranes started calling. Daring not to move a muscle – by now less of a worry given the early stages of hypothermia – we prayed for a direct hit. If, please God, the birds were to fly immediately above us, the recording would be in eardrum-shattering stereo. Judge for yourself. However, you need to be told one thing. When that first troubadour obliged with the mother of all reveilles above Magnus's microphones, there was an even louder – but outwardly silent – "YES!" from three motionless oversize possums.

That night we packed our bags. We had lodged for four days in simple comfort at Allucant, a cosy hostel built and run by Javier Manas and Litzan Campana, through which they hoped to promote – and thereby protect – the area. It felt as though we had gone bush, that it was time to saddle up the mare and cross those misty mountains. Before that, one question remained. I said, "Is Gallocanta and Allucant really the same word? In Northern Ireland we have Derry and Londonderry and they are the same place." Magnus, never one to miss a chance to shine, advanced his erudite Latin theory. "'Gallo' is chicken,

and 'canto' means chant: could the combination be analogous to Hensing in China or Cocksyodel in Holland?" For this polyglot attempt Litzan smiled in a pastoral capacity. Then he told us the true story. "Gallocanta is a Spanish name, a corruption of the original Allucant – which is Arabic. Commencing in 711, Arabs and Moroccan Berbers (collectively known as Moors) settled first southern Spain, and then all of the Iberian Peninsula and southwest France. Cordoba became their metropolis. It grew to become a city of a million people, grander than Constantinople – the greatest city in civilisation. Lights illuminated the streets and education was universal. There were 800 schools, colleges and a university. Islamic architecture, poetry and art enjoyed a golden age. It was the Moors who gave Allucant its beautiful name – and why we have chosen to revive it and keep it alive." Transfixed, we asked what it meant. He said, "The Place of Light." Perfect.

February 2008

Wouldn't it be great if it was like this all the time?

Who dares **wins**

Help! It's July, the month that feels like a hangover. The mudflats are bare, the sea is dead, bird song is over and self-respecting passerines are hiding their moulting bodies in dense undergrowth. A pity eclipse waterfowl don't do the same. Given the circumstances, weird turns are excusable but unlike you lot, looking at dragonflies or trapping moths doesn't do me any good at all.

Originally, I'd thought of writing just a few lines this month – *Birding from the Hip lite*: less to read, more time to go birding – and filling the rest of the page with an autumnal 'magic eye' scene of a Blackburnian Warbler on Blakeney Point. Alas, it was not to be. Apparently, the job of a columnist is to slug away even in demoralizing summer sunshine and conjure up images of grey skies over cool coasts with the whiff of migration in the air. Even the thought, dear reader, brings me close to tears. If only life was so simple. In the meantime, here is a story dredged up from memories of a long Indian summer of birding adolescence when boys were men and trespass was tantamount to terrorism.

Welcome to 1980s Belfast. Not a good time to be a teenager. The rubble and barbed wire, litter and sectarian graffiti and air of impoverishment are just streets away. Yet amid the sprawl of coastal reclamation works in dockland it is safe. There are no idle youths with beer and tattoos. Sadly, there are plenty of edgy cops.

"What the hell is going on here?"

"Just looking at birds, officer. I can show you a bird book to prove it."

"Is that a fact? Well, I have news for you. At this moment there are a few people" (he motioned toward the back of an army Landrover) "looking at *you* – but down the sight of a rifle." He was right, of course. Nabbed again. What was it to be this time?

To hardened trespassers, the procedure was familiar. It would involve (i) detention for some time and questioning at length, (ii) surrounded in a military pincer movement that would leave us unscathed but flush everything in sight and (iii) the rigmarole of names, addresses, driver's licence details, a fool's pardon and – if we were lucky – ten minutes grace to scan the lagoons before we had to vamoose and never return (ha-hah).

Why all the fuss? It had to do with the location of the reclamation pools. They were sandwiched between an oil refinery and the open waters of Belfast Lough. Moreover, the entire area was patrolled by heavily armed cops since it also contained an army

Be honest – if you caught this lot with telescopes and binoculars near a military base, would you ask them for ID or reach for your revolver?

base, ordnance depot, airstrip, Royal Navy berth, Short's missile factory (keep that to yourself) and just for good measure, 95 per cent of Northern Ireland's fuel supplies. In other words, we were birding in a McDonalds for terrorists.

The mud-splattered Fiat 127 putt-putted towards the bristling security of the main gate. Four scruffy figures look vacantly ahead, practised 'grey men' with no body language or eye contact to betray their motives. The driver nonchalantly holds up his forged RSPB membership card and the bozo at the checkpoint waves us through. Piece of cake.

"Wing-nut, I have to hand it to you. That move with the card is a cracker. Of course, it helps when you actually look like an SAS man instead of a former member of the Young Ornithologists' Club."

There was no challenge on the way out – because of the exhaustive check on the way in – so, except when detected by a vehicle patrol, it was usually possible to come and go with impunity. Bird-wise, the place was brilliant. A Pectoral Sandpiper, Roseate Tern, or Mediterranean Gull could usually be counted upon and apart from the frustration of being collared, you had the birds to yourself. In fact, the greatest threat to peace came, not from police but peers. "How do you guys get in? Every time I try, I am told that I need a special pass. I know you jammy sods don't have one, so how on Earth …"

Probably, the most risky manoeuvre of all was that performed to locate dozing rare gulls. A sleeping Ring-billed Gull could easily be overlooked among the massed ranks of other species, so someone was needed to break the skyline with arms raised

to 'shuffle the gull pack,' causing the horde to lift and settle in a different order.

It's funny how perceptions differ. A silhouette that to a gull looks like an oncoming raptor looks totally different to a police sergeant. Curiously, when he arrived, there was no interrogation – just a perfunctory request for names and addresses. He was almost friendly, but still a pain. Maybe some 'but you know we wouldn't harm a fly' bootlicking wouldn't go amiss? "Excuse me," I said. "We have been stopped lots of times. In fact, you've personally taken our details twice before. Surely by now you know who we are and why we sneak onto Belfast Harbour Estate? I know that what we have done is wrong and I am very sorry to waste valuable police time." I parrotted those lines like an air-steward going through a boring safety demonstration. He didn't respond immediately but I noticed a lot of boxes being left blank on his 'description of suspect vehicle' form.

"Well, it's like this," he began. "By the end of my shift I'm supposed to have a minimum of four entries in my incident book. Taxi-drivers without necessary security passes, lorry-drivers who try to get into depots past closing time – that kind of idiot. I'll level with you. There are a few dodgy geezers driving through this joint that are probably up to no good but I know you boys are OK. Somebody else can worry about them. You haven't the intelligence to be dangerous. You are harmless. Just conversationists or naturists or whatever you call yourselves."

"Twitchers," I volunteered, trying to sound like a helpful boy scout. "That's right - twits for short." (He thought that was funny. Even worse, he expected us to laugh – that we did, purely for advantage, of course.)

It was like finding the Russian fleet at anchor.

"Oh yes," he continued, "I need to examine that telescope. I wouldn't mind one like it myself – handy for looking at ferries coming up the lough. How far can you see with it?"

"It all depends," I said, wanting to extract some respect from the invigilator, "whether you mean day or night." He looked worried. He said, "I work shifts so night would be best." "In that case you are lucky," I assured him, "by day you can manage only 93 million miles but a damn sight further at night." "Wow!" he exclaimed. "You boys certainly take this game seriously." "It's the new model," I replied.

August 1995
Birdwatch

Oops!

The easiest exam I ever took was my driving rest. Unless a White-throated Needletail had appeared overhead and caused me to jump a red light in pursuit of it, I was, with hindsight, certain to turn in a virtuoso driving performance backed up with a Koran-like memorization of *The Highway Code*. The reason for this unbounded confidence was simple. I was 17, I regarded a driving license as a passport to freedom and I'd prepared myself accordingly. If I passed (and I did), I would be emancipated forever from a reliance on pedal power and hopeless public transport that went nowhere near birding hotspots.

The one minor detail that I hadn't considered in this post-driving test Utopia was, ahem, my lack of a car. Still, I was sure my dad wouldn't mind if I borrowed the family car from time-to-time, especially if I replaced the petrol I used. So was born the game of fuel tank brinkmanship, whereby neither of us left the other with more than a thimble-full of petrol. At the same time the annual mileage went through the roof when not just the four corners of Ireland were visited on birding trips but also the Scottish Highlands, Anglesey, Norfolk, Cornwall and even Shetland! This one-sided abuse of parental good offices finally came to an end when I got married, a turning point of deep significance for my dad, which he mentioned specifically in his wedding speech: "Today, after 10 long years of turmoil, I have lost a son but regained a car." God bless him.

Shush! There's a lot more turmoil that he doesn't know about. Nothing has been said about a litany of near misses, breakdowns and brushes with the law, or a string of hair-raising swerves and 50mph pirouettes, including some performed backwards on black ice. Oddly enough, one of the potentially gravest incidents occurred within days of passing the test. Its cause had a familiar theme – four pairs of eyes watching birds at the expense of everything else.

That day we were burning up our first flocks of Eiders on the Antrim coast and spotted an opportunity to get near the quarry by driving down a slipway and concealing the car among several boats that were parked on trailers close to the water's edge. The plan worked to perfection. Nearly 100 fantastic drakes, many calling and displaying, steamed right past the bonnet. Then we got even closer. This manoeuvre was spontaneous and a combined function of gravity, a steep slipway gradient and having parked on seaweed. I remember thinking at the time, "Why are all those boats moving?" until I realised that we were the mobile object. Everybody screamed, I hit the brakes; the car slewed sideways but continued its inexorable progress towards

Look on the bright side. The car's green and we're green. With any luck we'll blend in and the Polar Bears won't spot us.

Davy Jones's locker. There was nothing we could do except look forward to underside as well as upperside views of the Eiders. Before that happened there was a thump and a jolt and four terrified teenage birders found themselves spared. The car had collided with the back end of a boat. Not only were we safe, but also a rubber tyre dangling fortuitously over the stern had even saved the car's bodywork from damage. Phew!

My knowledge of auto mechanics is minimal and learned entirely as a consequence of breakdowns. The first time something goes wrong I won't have a clue how to fix it, but a second time – well, maybe. So it was in October 1987 when three of us twitched a Dusky Warbler in far-flung County Cork, 350 miles from home. We saw the bird brilliantly well and were in high spirits for the return leg of the journey. Then the clutch broke. We knew what to do – jam the car into top gear and keep going – but we had the whole of Ireland between Belfast and us. If we stopped once we'd be finished. How were we going to negotiate our way through towns, villages, red lights and Dublin's notorious city centre traffic? Furthermore, there was the slight problem of Basher Barnes who lived in Dublin and was expecting to be dropped off there.

Realistically, we didn't expect to last long, but a combination of judicious speed control and copious blasting of the horn got us through. Approaching Dublin, the biggest difficulty was no longer dodging pedestrians in the middle of level crossings, but having to let Basher out. As decision time loomed, selfish motives took hold. We gave him two choices. Travel to Belfast and catch a train home the next morning – or jump. He thought we were joking until we told him he could borrow our hats and gloves to protect his face and hands. Then we practiced Dambuster-like

slow deceleration runs alongside soft grassy verges until he plucked up enough courage to bale out of the back seat. He did it and so became known as Basher Barnes-Wallis.

The exhilaration of an exciting day's birding takes you only so far. Long night drives, wet roads and hunger pose dangers to which a tired driver may be oblivious. These factors explain what I did one fateful night. I was bleary-eyed from an eight-hour seawatch and felt myself nodding off at the wheel. Through pouring rain and darkness I remember seeing lights that materialized into a filling station, phone box and, to the wonder of all, a café that was still open. Instinctively I swung the car around and abandoned it close to the café door. I dashed inside out of the rain and tucked into a late-night feast of grease and tea. What a score.

Half an hour later I felt wide-awake, which helped prepare me for the shock to come. Two red-faced policemen burst through the door and made straight for me. My legs turned to jelly as I confirmed that, yes, I did own the car outside. What had I done? I guessed they'd been following me and I had probably clocked up several speeding offences over the previous hour or more. I decided to throw myself at their mercy and plead guilty to everything, but first I had better hear the charges. It emerged that, half an hour before, they had received a call from a distressed pensioner. The caller, an aged petrol station proprietor, had been trapped inside a phone box by an idiot who'd parked tight against the phone box door. Luckily the old boy got the car's registration number and phoned the cops. "Could you move your car sir?" "Right away, officer," I said, delighted.

October 1998
Birdwatch

My life with a **jerk**

Mrs McGeehan *reveals some home truths*

It was the spark that lit the fuse. A casually overheard remark that had an effect far greater than he ever imagined. The house was a mess, the kids wild and I was bone-tired after struggling through three hours of ironing. He had been yakking on the phone like an old fishwife for the last 40 minutes. Then I heard him say it. "Hey Dominic, I'll be too busy birding this October to write my column. I'll need a month off."

TOO BUSY BIRDING…NEED A MONTH OFF! These were his exact words, spoken as though he was buckling under some sort of *pressure*. What about me, the person who cleans his house and raises his children; am I not entitled to a break? The thought never entered his head. So I've taken over his slot for October. He'll be on Cape Clear Island when he reads this. Hopefully the first inkling he'll get of what I've done is when he meets bunches of birders talking in whispers – about him – and murmuring, "My God, I didn't think he was such a bad husband, LET ALONE A CREEP."

We met between his birding trips. He'd see me when he came back from Scotland, when he came back from seawatching in Mayo, when he came back from Israel. He was different then. Full of stories and usually suntanned. My mother was so

impressed she even called him Lawrence of Arabia. Now she calls him Saddam.

The first alarm bells sounded on the night of our wedding rehearsal. The same day a lost Elegant Tern was discovered in County Down. He phoned at six o'clock to say he couldn't make the rehearsal. I yelled at him that I was supposed to be the most elegant thing in his life. "Right now you come an extremely close second to a tern," was the reply. He thought this sounded sympathetic, although he did promise not to try and get the stupid bird on his 'Wedding Day list'.

We'd planned our romantic Austrian honeymoon months in advance: the Tyrol, Innsbruck, Salzburg, Vienna. When we arrived I also discovered there was a hidden agenda: Alpine Accentor, Snow Finch, Great Bustard. I was abandoned at the top of the Brenner Pass while he tramped across mountaintops for hours. He came back sick and exhausted. Even worse, he'd 'dipped'. "A little bird has been feeding young in the car park wall all afternoon," I told him, hoping it might cheer him up. "In fact, here it comes again." For a second I thought he'd become violently ill but it was only a reaction to a "barely tickable view of an alleged Snow Finch". Hmm! Shortly afterwards, I spotted the Alpine Accentor

"It takes photographs like this – of the kids, plus me for scale – to remind Anthony that he has other responsibilities in life, not just birding."

hopping along a crash barrier. He managed the bustards all by himself – but they were big enough even for him to see.

Married life began at the worst time of the year for me – autumn. First he didn't trust me to remember phone messages. "Write all the words down," was his dumb advice. I did, but that didn't help. He blew his top (and then ridiculed me for weeks) when I wrote: "Rare wee dear in Cork."

Now I ask for precise spellings. And what do I get? "Dave phoned to say he had a black, red, and pink foot." Another night saw a major panic when several people left the same message: "RING BILL GULL IN BELMULLET." I couldn't understand his puzzled reaction, followed by *inactivity*. Said he didn't know Bill Gull – did he not leave a number? He doesn't like to talk about that one. Not even his mates know the real reason why he took two days to see Ireland's first Ring-billed Gull.

Deceit, false promises and selfishness come naturally to Anthony. In the past we'd go away on *my* weekends off, maybe to Wexford or Cork. He'd say, "It'll be relaxing, quiet and scenic – you will get to see the birds too. And I used to. Then, just as I'd be watching Ringed Plovers (my favourite bird) he'd hear about a rarity. In 1983 it was a Yellow-breasted Bunting on Cape Clear Island. Zoom. We're off. Dash 100 miles to the ferry. Walk two miles uphill. Find the field. Search for the bird. He has it – in a flock of Yellowhammers. "Can I see it?" No chance. He's hogging the telescope – *in case it flies, you understand* – nothing to do with him being selfish! The Yellowhammers were nicer anyway.

Rarities turn my husband into a werewolf. I hate them. The rarer they are, the worse he gets. He suffers terrible PMT (pre-

Nice picture, although the meaning is lost on the photographer.

Of course, I can't win anyway. If he doesn't go (because I won't let him) then he sulks or hauls himself around like a Spermless Whale.

Nowadays, I make him earn his birding time. Washing dishes equals an hour out; doing the shopping equals half a day; and, for just being nice and paying me some attention, up to a whole day. He calls this a credit system. I call it adulthood.

Has he any redeeming qualities? Well, he's 36 but still in his teens and the kids like him (similar mental age – temporarily in their case). Plus, he never seems to be bored, wants to live forever and doesn't want to go to heaven: something about there being no birds there. I wonder where gulls go when they die? I'm sure he would like it there. Come to think of it, might there be a few Ringed Plovers there too?

October 1993
Birdwatch

megatick tension). His stomach is bad and he becomes irrational. In the past he has dropped flasks, attempted to put diesel in the car, left his binoculars at home and, once, told me that he still loved me!

More than anything else, I dread the weekends. I know he'll want to go birding on Sunday but instead of being pleasant, helpful or *a good parent* during the week – to compensate for his absences from home – he resorts to trickery. Such as having one of his scheming friends phone me and lie about keeping a space on a trip for him: to make me feel guilty.

One of
the boys

Like a great ocean wave crashing on a shore, October almost always begins with a slam. In 1992, the shock waves reverberated from Orkney to Cork. First a Siberian Thrush was trapped at dusk on North Ronaldsay and then a cruising Soft-plumaged Petrel almost grazed the rocks at the tip of Galley Head. There were banner headlines before the Golden Month was even 24 hours old.

What a start. That night the question, "Have you heard what's on North Ronaldsay?" must have sparked a thousand reactions to someone's great luck and – for the fortunate few – a chance to share in it. Even for the masses that wouldn't get to see the thrush, its arrival stirred thoughts of mythical birds on the loose in our small part of the Northern Hemisphere. Indoors, news is always second-hand. Outdoors, miraculous events occur. Where do you look? Given a fortuitous combination of weather, place and time – and among the next thirty days there might be occasions that would call for celebrations, become famous anniversaries or leave memories that would last a lifetime. Anything could happen.

Suddenly the weather settled into a pattern that quickly became a rut. A massive cold air circulation developed and nothing shifted it. Some good birds would doubtless arrive, but if the big chill persisted then autumn migration was going to be a famine not a feast.

Nevertheless, unexpected change could come at any moment and there was always the chance of discovering lingering gems from September's glut of easterly winds. Optimism in the face of adversity. That is what it felt like at the time.

Ten days into a birdless October, a perceptive Kent birder claimed Ireland's first Isabelline Wheatear late on a Saturday evening at Mizen Head, over the sea from Cape Clear Island. Struck down by a lack of boats, I was one of a number of Young Turks marooned on Cape Clear until Monday. We did our best to create chaos out of confusion. In no time at all – five minutes to be exact – blind scepticism made some more doubtful of the bird's identification than they had been five minutes before. Others issued detailed instructions to 'low listers' not stuck on Cape Clear. Like members of a Scottish women's curling team, they were despatched with identification brooms to sweep the bird's path clear of impediments by confirming a few diagnostic features. They did it. It was one. Sunday night

October 1992, Mizen Head, Cork, Ireland. An era of no birdlines, mobile phones or text messages. Irish birders were different then - a lot hairier too. Inset: the Isabelline Wheatear that drew the crowd.

prayers reflected a new realism – please Lord, let the bird stay until Monday.

Hence, as well as cameras and notebooks, a bottle of Moet & Chandon nestled among the optical armour that wound its way to Mizen Head. Would the Isabelline Wheatear be there? It was – and received a welcome fit for Nigel Mansell. That evening a merry band of birders returned to Cape Clear. The last mainland pubs in Baltimore enjoyed some hasty trade before the mail boat sailed.

That appeared to be how the story ended: a good yarn to brag about in lean birding times, over future pints or on long car journeys to kindred souls who would love to have been there. It was a happy day without incident - apart from Luigi's exhaust pipe clattering along the road and then detaching itself from the car and everyone pretending that he had hit a rabbit and convincing him the car sounded fine (no one wanted to tell him his wake looked like a scene from the Gulf War in case he stopped to repair the damage and we missed the boat).

Nothing did outshine the Isabelline and memories of it probably helped keep Stuart McKee peaceable when he left Cape Clear a week later but arrived on the mainland minus his car keys. Home was 400 miles away. A panicky phone call back to the island initiated a search but produced nothing.

And so it was that a local barman noticed a burly group of Northern Irish birders looking for ways to break into a Ford Sierra. He asked the obvious question. Of course they'd lost the keys. Then maybe the bunch that had been left in his bar the previous Sunday was theirs? Great! He'd got the keys! Well, sort of. He had the keys then. Now they were in the local police station.

Baltimore is a small town with no part further than a walk up the street. However, when the police station is shut, the sergeant is out of town. Stuart's hopes had been raised and then dashed. He reported back to the barman. As is usual in Ireland, there is always someone who knows where people are, and the sergeant's whereabouts were quickly discovered. He was at a funeral ten miles away.

Philip, a fellow birder, drove Stuart there. The two of them stood near the church gates and awaited the arrival of both cortege and keyholder. When the hearse and mourners paused at the gates the undertaker motioned for a change of pall-bearers. In such situations a long face and solemn expression, caused by thoughts of a delayed journey home and missing keys, go a long way to inadvertently suggesting kinship or at least personal ties with the deceased. Maybe that's why Philip's and Stuart's shoulders were tapped to carry the coffin, which they duly hoisted into position and carried steadfastly up the aisle, mindful to keep in step with the cadence of the oratorio and to remain downcast in case a blood relative looked them tearfully in the eye.

Not until requiem mass was ended and they had finally waved goodbye to the sergeant did their powers of speech recover sufficiently to tell their story to some long-suffering passengers and thence the ornithological mass media.

Remember October 1992? Wasn't that the year Stuart had to carry a coffin before he got his car keys back? He was down in Cork looking for a rare bird. Now, what was it again?

February 1993
Birdwatch

Kids' stuff

Over here people are still talking about the dreadful 'flu that hit hard in January. Whole tiers of government were brought to their knees by the situation, which was made worse by those folk who were healthy deciding to take their traditional 'sick week' early, thereby avoiding the added pressure at work. Indirectly, the epidemic also led to a crisis in the McGeehan household when a neighbour asked me at short notice to fill a lecture slot for her church, the pre-arranged speaker having been laid low by the bug.

The problem was a clash with the wife's weekly karate class, which requires me to stay at home and mind the kids (ages six and 10). Under normal circumstances I make considerable efforts to get out of standing up in public and boring hapless victims to sleep, but this time a sense of good neighbourliness and the possibility of scoring some Brownie points with God tipped the balance. I agreed to do the talk: Birds & Bile. The queasy content was a compendium of anecdotes and tales of seabird encounters off the Irish coast during the course of several pelagic trips. However, I would have to bring the kids along. That worried me. I could shine them up, put them through a crash course in manners and good behaviour and park them in the front row wedged between two responsible adults, but would they sit at peace for a whole hour? Their previous personal best, about 50 seconds, didn't inspire confidence. I blackmailed them with the prospect of 99s after the show, but I still felt edgy.

Time for the sermon. The congregation's minister, who expressed a pastoral fervour for all things made by the Almighty, introduced me. He then went on to whip up a good head of collective eagerness and anticipation before finally announcing the talk's title as 'Birds & the Bible', by Andrew McGuigan.

When I said, "Those of a queasy disposition should look away now," the kids were transfixed. "Wow!" they said, "think of the splat if you jumped into that stuff – never mind the brilliant smell."

The reverend left me with a difficult task. I had to pull off a big mood swing from belief in eternal happiness with a loving God to the paganism of 20 foul-mouthed birders crammed together on a boat laden with barrels of rancid fish on, invariably, the Sabbath. The first slide was a map of the North Atlantic, which offered an escape route. I used it to drone on and on about a falsified connection between 'The birds of the heavens and the fish of the sea' (Psalm 8:8) and waffled about the longevity of seabirds (a further link with the audience), and the fantastic migratory feats that birds perform. Manx Shearwater, a species most people would have seen off the local coastline, came in for special treatment. Notably the individual, which, as part of a homing experiment in 1954, was transported 3,050 miles from Skokholm to Boston, Massachusetts, and then released. Twelve days later it was back in its burrow, having beaten by 10 hours the letter posted from Boston reporting its liberation!

This was well and good, but it only postponed the inevitable seasick shots of wet and bedraggled adults with gaping mouths and ribbons of toilet tissue clinging to un-wiped vomit on the leeward side of sagging jaws. Even worse, one victim was a local schoolteacher well known by the kids and probably familiar to some in the gathering. In the end there wasn't a shred of evangelism to be extracted from the closing images. It was as though the opening hymns had given way to hell and damnation, but at least it was over. Afterwards, people were very kind and shook my hand to show how much they had enjoyed the talk. Some offered advice on motion sickness, which led to a group discussion on coping with diarrhoea, nausea, dehydration and other debilitating effects of the present 'flu, all of which made me feel that perhaps I had been of some service after all.

Of course, the real pundits were the two I took home in the car. I asked them, "So, kids, what did you think?" It was strange to be a dad and feel so powerless: about to be judged by your own offspring without inhibitions or charity. The first response was just about reassuring. They said, "Oh, not that bad." I said, "So, what were the good bits?" That opened the floodgates. Out poured a line-by-line repetition of the goriest stories of the night. How Stuart fell into the ship's hold in total darkness and nearly broke a leg. About Davy waking up to find that he had shared a bunk with a rat. And the midnight raid on our chum supply that was believed to contained sealed packets of drugs – when the customs officer dredged through the barrels with his bare hands and fished out nothing more sinister than cod heads. But not a word about birds. "Is that it?" I said, "What about the rest?" "Mmm," they replied, "not great. The maps were the worst – that was school stuff. But the stories were cool. Even the people asleep beside us woke up during them."

That was in January. Since then they have remembered the shearwaters, petrels, skuas and terns in lasting detail. Their homework is full of embellished tales of near-fatalities on the high seas, and occasionally a little about those members of the audience whom they were forced to sit beside. Kids are unpredictable beings: highly observant and equipped with fertile minds that are not easily roused by parental stimulation. This time they seem to have latched onto birds because the blood and guts were left in, instead of being replaced with sugary storylines. On the other hand, there could be a maternal factor at work, of which I am unaware. I'll keep you posted.

May 1997
Birdwatch

Twitchers
are human too

It took only four words to reorganize an evening, a weekend - and very nearly a marriage. My wife's yellow post-it was stuck prominently on my bottle of Grecian 2000. "WESTERN SANDPIPER, NORTH SLOB." The effect was akin to sudden weightlessness and the loss of power. My brain, now emptied of life's other ballast, sought the one thing that might have a calming effect – more information. Who saw it? Was it *really* Ireland's first Western Sandpiper?

A frantic phone call to Dublin answered the first question and rendered the second irrelevant. Killian Mullarney had found it on a drained duck pond at the North Slob wildfowl reserve in Wexford. Views were reported as excellent; the bird was a pristine juvenile and it was there until late evening. Eek!

Clearly this was going to be a major twitch, and probably an unprecedented one in Irish terms (where, to assemble a crowd of 30 at a rarity, you would have to add in driving spouses and the odd hitch-hiker). Plans had already been laid by just about everybody in the country to be in Wexford by dawn. I couldn't be one of them. Debilitated by an attack of 'some of us have to go to work you know' syndrome, I couldn't attempt a rendezvous until the following evening.

The next day's reports began with tales of a mercurial Western tied to erratic Dunlin flocks, but by midday rising pulse rates had been matched by a rise in life lists. It took until lunchtime the following day before I clapped eyes on it.

When the diminutive star finally appeared, the waiting throng had swelled to nearly 200 birders, most arriving hot-foot overnight from Britain and quite a few making u-turns at the Rutland Bird Fair. Ninety minutes of uninterrupted views were enough to beat any cup final. But try telling that to relatives, workmates and worst of all, the media.

A 36-year old man with a responsible job, wife, family and mortgage has a credibility problem when it comes to explaining the excitement and wonder caused by a small bird that spends much of its time sticking its face into wet mud. Communication skills go only so far in conveying the fascination of something rare, especially when the illustration summoned as supporting evidence happens to be the one in Heinzel, Fitter and Parslow's field guide. Exasperating, isn't it?

Try a different approach. Reach for Lars Jonsson's paintings of stints and peeps in *British Birds* (July 1984) and sow the seeds of understanding. Let uninitiated eyes gaze upon the copious fine print of Peter Grant's text. Mention that in subtlety there is beauty. Draw a few parallels and explain the thrill of discovery in being able to recognize birds from all corners of the Earth close to home. You'll strike a chord: everyone feels a certain humility at the globetrotting abilities of birds.

What about introducing the significance of vagrancy patterns or the worth of bird identification for 'conservation' reasons? Each has a place but, in explaining the adrenalin rush of something as absorbing as a rarity, those are the worst flags of convenience. They introduce an elitism that obscures the simple gut reaction of enjoying birds, rare or otherwise. It is a satisfaction that should be communicated in terms of awe and wonder – rather than couched in scientific argot.

Sure, like most of the others, I was engrossed in checking the Western's features, such as the extent of rufous on the crown and scapulars, its bill shape and length, primary projection and the feasibility of seeing its unique foot webbing. All part of the process of learning, cross-referencing and (hopefully) being able to re-employ identification features in future.

But what if the next rare bird is a Wandering Albatross with no attendant identification problems, or a scarce migrant that I've seen many times before? For me rarity comes at the end of a scale along which ordinary becomes special, regular becomes unusual, familiar becomes new and straightforward becomes challenge. Such a scale accommodates most of what I enjoy in birding, so when the strands combine it is

bound to amount to a special occasion. Beer is fine all of the time but it is nice to drink champagne occasionally.

December 1992
Birdwatch

Who said that something rare has to be spectacular? Does the Dalai Lama do flips and rolls?

The **Orange Order**

If you're Irish it can be hard to warm to the Dutch. That's an unkind thought I'm glad to get off my chest, but there are good reasons for it. Back in 1690, Protestant King William of Orange came over here from Holland and knocked the stuffing out of a bunch of Catholic relatives of mine and we're still a bit sore about it. Especially as the crowd of Scots he hired to help him are still here and have turned into insufferable supporters of Glasgow Rangers who are currently 10 points clear at the top of the Scottish Premier Division, aided and abetted by Dick Advocaat as manager with three Dutch players in the squad. Apparently, they don't enjoy having to wear kilts at official team functions, such as at charitable dinners where only haggis is served. Well, good.

Some recompense was made in the last century thanks to the arrival in Ireland of Dutch drainage engineers. Under their direction, a part of the muddy shoreline of Lough Foyle, Ulster's largest estuary, was transformed into a mini Flevoland. No doubt many Pale-bellied Brent Geese and Wigeon were made homeless into the bargain, but the new agricultural land is among the richest in the country. How did this save Dutch bacon? I'll tell you.

On a cold grey windy day in October 1983 I was sheltering behind a dyke bordering the expanse of new fields. Peering across the windmill-less landscape I noticed a goose-like bird cruising low and close to the ground. As it got closer, it caused a strange reaction among flocks of Lapwing and Golden Plover. The effect was akin to someone screaming, "run for your life." The birds were panicking; hurling themselves into the air like shrapnel. I wondered about my identification and then, wing beat by steady powerful wing beat, the enormous truth hit me. It wasn't a goose; it was a falcon. This explained the terror. On it came with Cruyff-like precision until, in a supreme moment, it twisted its head and looked down at me in an icy stare as if to say, "take cover, pea-brain." Such was my first encounter with a Gyr on a Dutch-built polder in Northern Ireland. I said, "Thank you Holland for creating the habitat." Dutch ingenuity recognized. Then things took another nose-dive in 1995, on 13 December, to be precise.

That night, in the emotion-charged atmosphere of Anfield, the Dutch football team cast a dark shadow on our X-ray of national well-being. Ireland, a footballing leprechaun with big hearts and guts to match, faced the mighty Dutch, inventors of total football with players interchanging positions at astonishing speed. Not only was this tie the decider in Ireland's chances of qualifying for the European Championship in 1996, but it was also billed as a game that

A hundred years ago, when Dutch drainage engineers made polders in Ireland, they inadvertently created perfect hunting habitat for a vagrant Gyrfalcon. This has gone some way to making up for earlier sins.

Jack Charlton's team had to win to keep the manager in a job.

I watched the match with my mother. At kick-off she sat unblinking, silent as a holy statue, with a little speech balloon over her head containing the words: "Holy Mary, Mother of God, pray for our brave footballers now until the full-time whistle, amen." Throughout her life she has avoided sin and foul language but it was exciting to see her come close to it, especially in the thirtieth minute when Kluivert evaded Phil Babb's lunge and flashed a low left-foot shot across Kelly and into the far corner of the Irish goal. Out came the rosary beads; a sure sign that an equalizer would be along in a minute.

However, after half-time the future began to look anything but green. When Paul McGrath's volley missed the Dutch crossbar by a distance shorter than Sinead O'Connor's haircut, Mother Superior glowered at a picture of the Pope on the wall and implored him to: "Hurry up and do something, for Christ's sake." And maybe John Paul II did do something, for Van der Sar in the Dutch goal seemed hypnotized. He stood rooted to his spot, as though transfixed by a psychokinetic force. Despite this helping hand from the Vatican, Ireland's problem was that they didn't have a single shot on target. In the ninetieth minute Kluivert got a second goal and it was all over. I cried; my mother cried. She left the room. I sensed the defeat had gone deep, perhaps undermining her faith in the Almighty. I found her in tears in the greenhouse, defiantly spraying the sprouting tulips with Agent Orange. When I told her that Kluivert's Christian name was Patrick and that, having Irish grandparents, he should rightfully have been playing for Ireland, she cheered up a little. She said, "Never

mind, son. It wasn't the team's fault. That's what comes of having an Englishman as manager. God told me it was an ill omen."

What followed was pure *This is your Life*, although the television was off by now. Waves of recollection started to well up from somewhere deep. Nothing dramatic such as heavy snowfalls, Christmas mornings, or watching a neighbour's house burn down, but simple influences absorbed by overhearing grownup conversations. In those days parents still talked a lot about 'the war'. I used to listen, late at night, when they thought I was fast asleep. I'd hear them murmuring downstairs and crawl out onto the landing, lean over the banister and imagine it was the edge of a parapet, below which lay a pit of bad news. The bad news seeped under the kitchen door and solidified like a thick drapery of candle wax in the hallway below me. With my resolve stiffened in daylight, I asked my mum who started the war. Bad people, she said, mainly Germans and Italians. But the pope saved us. Later I found out that 'Our Holy Father' was Italian and for years assumed that the wartime pope, Pius XII, had been a double agent, fighting for the allies behind enemy lines, a bit like Richard Burton in *Where Eagles Dare*. A more exciting memory was watching the 1966 World Cup, especially the final. My dad became really excited, and the pair of us got quite carried away watching England slug it out against West Germany in injury time. Everybody was jubilant when they won. Well, not quite everyone. My mum was the exception. At the time hers was a lone voice, a siren Churchill bulldog predicting a grim outcome. She said, "God help us now that England have won the World Cup – we will never hear the end of it." And, as mothers tend to be, she was right, of course.

In a way this sums up the strength of our national character. We may have a strong weakness for the drink and indulge in what to everyone else is motiveless fighting, but we are blessed with an ability to blame our misfortunes on the English, thereby preserving good relations with everyone else, even the Dutch. Take ornithology. Just as you coined total football, Holland is the only country to have enshrined altruism as a core value underpinning its national birding scene. *Dutch Birding* is a non-profit-making journal with no paid staff, the birdline in Holland raises funds for the Dutch Birding Association; and a Dutch committee for avian systematics, itself part of the DBA, maintains a watchful eye on contemporary scientific research and pronounces on taxonomic matters accordingly. To paraphrase the stirring words of President Abraham Lincoln, the Dutch have achieved 'Government of the people, by the people, for the people'.

Yet, listen to some sections of the British birding establishment these days and you will often hear the view expressed that the Dutch, in embracing the Phylogenetic Species Concept as the foundation for taxonomic thinking, have gone too far. The worrying thing about this opinion is that it is based more on a peculiar brand of fossilized conservatism rather than a real grasp of what's going on outdoors. But don't take my word for it. Look tomorrow at the plumage, structure, calls and behaviour of Caspian Gull *Larus cachinnans* and ask yourself: how come the British Ornithologists' Union think this is the same species as Herring Gull?

Thankfully, the balance of support for the PSC is tipping the right way. Indeed, the concept has been enshrined as an important legal principle in Irish law. In a recent test case a defendant successfully avoided payment of an old debt when he used the PSC, backed up with scientific tests and forensic evidence, to show that the process of change is endemic in the natural world with new species evolving constantly. On this basis he demonstrated that, through cell replacement, the physical structure of *Homo sapiens* is wholly renewed every seven years meaning that, under PSC rules, he was no longer 'diagnosably' the man he once was and, therefore, didn't have to pay back the money.

Which leads me to clear up a small misunderstanding. It has been fun writing these words for *Dutch Birding* and I've done so in response to a verbal request from Gerald O'Reel (I assume there's some Irish blood in his veins). However, I'm puzzled by what he meant when he said, "write for the president." Maybe the word was 'right', not 'write'? Me, right for president of DBA? Naturally I accept, if only because my mother will be pleased to hear that she has a son in charge of an Orange Order. Then it really will be payback time.

February 2000
Dutch Birding

Bless me
Father

Summer colds are the worst. Steaming hot drinks and wrapping up warm to ward off 'the elements' just aren't possible when late August temperatures don't dip below 20 degrees centigrade. Deprived of even psychological support, you sniff, cough and swear through days of misery. Then you try some mind over matter. An early night and – purely for medicinal reasons – hot whiskies. These are just the circumstances to guarantee a midnight phone call about a rare bird.

"Oh, hi George. No, I wasn't in bed. No, not a sore throat exactly – just a bit of a cold." For cold sufferers, the news was bad – a rumour of a possible dowitcher. The only thing that was certain was the location, a brackish marsh near Killough village, a five-mile detour off my route to work.

Now what? Could I steel myself for an early rise and dress, feed and prepare two young children for school and pinch an hour's birding time before work? A bit unfair on the kids? The decision: a minor inconvenience. GO FOR IT. Zoom. "Everybody in the car, remember the lunchboxes. Seat-belts on, mind that door - BAM!" Too late. For injecting just a little too much pace into the morning's proceedings, I paid a high price. Thinking,

understandably, that some sort of emergency was happening, the kids slammed the car door shut on my thumb. Nevertheless, 40 minutes later I was nearing the target location. A security checkpoint hove into view. "I'm sorry sir, there is a bomb in Killough this morning and the area is sealed off." There are times when luck seems to go AWOL, patience comes to an end and expletives aren't printable. This was one of them.

A U-turn and work? Did I really want to persevere? The argument that runs, "Well, you've come this far, so why not?" made my mind up. One last try. I detoured around the coast, made the most of a low tide and waded across mudflats, followed by enforced leaping of ditches to bypass the village. By the time I reached a raised vantage point overlooking the marsh, I felt like I'd conquered more landforms than Sir Edmund Hillary. And what did I see? Nothing. No sign of a dowitcher. A Black-tailed Godwit and several Common Snipes – could one of these have been the source of the story? Fifteen minutes. I'll give it 15 minutes and then I'll have to go. A brief time for a pendulum to swing. Presently, I found a Garganey and watched it swim into some cover, from where it dislodged a dowitcher!

'Divine intervention' is sometimes cited when it comes to the discovery of a rare bird. However, in the case of this dowitcher, God was right in there at the deep end.

A pleasing result but not a perfect one. The bird was in summer plumage, at 400 metres range, and 15 minutes was up. At 30x through the telescope, it looked like a Long-billed Dowitcher but I couldn't exclude the possibility that it might be a Short-billed. I was not going to fluff the identification. There was nothing else for it, I would have to return later and somehow try to get close enough to check diagnostic plumage features.

So far so good. The early start, a cold, even a bomb (later defused) hadn't deflected me. It seems as though birders will put up with a lot just to see a bird. But how much? The dowitcher had anaesthetized the throbbing pain in my thumb but now that was back with a vengeance. By lunchtime, painkillers and ice were having no effect. By late afternoon I was in an accident and emergency ward at Downpatrick hospital. The lady doctor grimaced at me when I held up my sore digit. Looking at her body language, the word 'pathetic' seemed to be flashing through her brain. She opened her handbag and fished out a cigarette lighter. Was I going to be offered a final fag before the big operation? No. She straightened a paper clip, heated its tip with the lighter's flame and snapped, "Quick, give me your thumb." So much for counselling. Cuticle and underlying skin were seared and a geyser of blood spurted through the hole in my nail. "There you are," she said, "not key-hole, but kebab surgery." I was free to go. Theoretically, I had plenty of time to fulfil important family commitments – collect the kids from their granny's and pick up my wife from work. *Or maybe I could go back and look for the dowitcher?* How low was I prepared to stoop? What would you have done?

Granny McNally, my mother-in-law, is one of life's saints. The soul of kindness. She is Belfast's answer to Mother Teresa. Surely I couldn't bring myself to lie to her? "Hello, Mrs McNally, I'm in casualty in Downpatrick hospital." Gasp. "I am about to have a crushed thumbnail lanced." "God love you!" "It's all right Mrs McNally, I'll try to be brave but I can't collect the kids tonight and…" "Oh, don't worry about that. I'll manage. You poor thing."

There you are, my secret's out. I told a pork pie so that I could see a rare bird. Having told you what I did, I'm glad to have got that sin off my chest. After such deceit I speculated that my come-uppance might be not seeing the dowitcher. Maybe if I promised to God that I would confess the truth later, then the bird would still be there? Okay, I promised. And it was.

A day that had begun disastrously finished in heaven. Following an hour-long cautious approach, I began to have suspicions about the dowitcher's skills of identification. I was sure I knew what it was (a Long-billed) but what did it think I was – a Moose, Caribou or inquisitive Grizzly? I must have resembled something from its breeding grounds for it accepted me completely. Eventually both of us were side by side in oozy mud, it stuffing its face and me wondering how much longer I could stand the cold water lapping around my knees. I thought to myself, "Lucky you had the presence of mind to take your trousers off before wading into the marsh. No point in ruining a perfect alibi with mud-stained trousers." Oh no! I looked at the muddy mess of my bandaged thumb. Damn. "All right God, about that promise: you win."

December 1993
Birdwatch

No more
Mr Nice Guy

Cats. I hate them. They are to wild birds what the month of December is to Turkeys. Apart from the grim toll they have already taken of the world's island-nesting seabirds and endemic landbirds, the statistics for the carnage they wreak on garden birds are appalling. In 1999, there were an estimated eight million cats in the United Kingdom. Based on survey trials conducted by the British Trust for Ornithology, each of 50 monitored cats caught, on average, a bird a week. The point of the survey was to test the reduction in birds killed by cats fitted with collars that bleep. The outcome? Fitting the nation's cats with bleepers might reduce the estimated number of birds killed annually by cats from 50 million to 20 million.

On a more personal level, prowling moggies deprive me of the pleasure of feeding ground-dwelling birds in my own garden, so I've planted a copse of bird-attracting trees instead. These keep the winter's crop of Lesser Redpolls, Siskins and tits well clear of the clutches of the enemy below. Still, my heart sinks and my blood rises each breeding season when I see parties of young ground-feeding songbirds – especially Song Thrushes – mauled to death by well-fed 'pets': affluent cats, not poor starved wretches hunting for food. That really makes me mad.

The hunting grounds of these feline fiends, suburban gardens, is also the haunt of something rather special – wintering Blackcaps. I love their coy, smart looks and general elusiveness. Elusive, that is, until I discovered that they have a soft spot for halved apples. Soon I had a veritable treasure trail of Marks & Sparks' fruit leading inexorably to a Red Delicious impaled on a log. The log was a prop arranged at minimum focusing distance from the kitchen door. All I needed now for a photo opportunity was some Saturday morning sunshine: in other words, my wife's favourite shopping weather. That's why I was looking after two young children (aged six and three) as well as trying to operate a camera.

Compared to the heirs, I had more problems with marauding Starlings and bad light. Incessant log watching eventually paid dividends. I managed several photographs of a sprightly male Blackcap until a grey blur materialized through the camera viewfinder. Fur! Before it had time to draw claws I reached for ammunition (a rock-hard Granny Smith) and wrenched the door open. The son-of-a-bitch scarpered, I took aim and the apple flew as though unleashed by a West Indian fast bowler. But instead of thudding into the wannabe assassin it splatted against a tree, missing the target, although showering it with pulp.

Then the guilt started. *How could I be so cruel?* Enticing a beloved Blackcap within inches of certain death? Its demise would have been my fault. Terrible. Ashamed, I removed all apples that were less than six feet above the ground. Worse was to come.

"Dad, dad, come quick, something's the matter with Tom." It was my daughter's distraught voice. However Thomas, her younger brother, seemed fine. Well, guess who Tom turned out to be? The cat. Maybe his surname was Cruise? It should have been, for he was putting on a performance fit to win an Oscar. There he was, squirming on the ground, his cynical attention-seeking corrupting the mind of a child while he licked tit-bits of apple from his coat. Not only *eating at my expense* but also forging ahead in the battle to convert a new generation of hearts and minds to cat worship. What a nerve - indoctrinating my own kids!

"Can't we bring him in dad, he must be cold and hungry and …" I could sense the tears getting ready to flow, especially if I said "No." Do that and I'd risk losing another PR round to the tabby terror. I was being undermined, haemorrhaging moral high ground and, at this point, likely to look a heartless parent whose lack of Christian charity was exposed by – *a cat.*

Oh boy. The damned thing had me on the ropes and by the sound of its latest manipulative *meows* it knew it. Summoning all the hypocritical powers of persuasion that I could muster, I explained that cats are (allegedly) warm-blooded animals that live outdoors. If we brought him in he'd feel trapped and frightened, poor thing. But, just to prove my concern, I would open the back door and see. A perfect strategy: call his bluff and be ready for a second strike to boot. I left the kids on lookout and walked towards the door, surreptitiously grabbing more ammo en route. As expected, all it took was one glimpse of me in imminent firing mode and he was off. Hopefully aware that, by the end of the morning's proceedings, the score was two lives forfeited to me and no bird breakfast for him.

So, by a whisker, I didn't lose face. But I will have to do something about the kids' misplaced sympathies. That night's bedtime stories were Peter *and the Cat*, followed by a new version of Little Red Riding Hood featuring a wicked cat dressed up as Granny. Before that I decided to bow to requests to take them to the park, with the added treat of hiring some Tom and Jerry videos on the way home. "Yeah! Great idea, dad." I thought so too, purrfect in fact.

March 1994
Birdwatch

A Blackcap in winter. Nine out of ten cats prefer them.

Shore
wars

A high-tide nap is such a major item on a shorebird's agenda that it will settle for any surroundings that provide one. Even a firing range. Nearly 1,000 Redshanks were hunkered down on the perimeter walls of the army camp and although the hail of lead and exploding mortars was directed away from them, the din and aftershocks were well up on the Richter scale. Still they stood on; resolute, one-legged, and apart from the occasional sentry, mostly headless; safe behind the impregnable perimeter fence despite having nothing white to wave. By now I know what they know. If they fly to roost inside the base, neither man nor beast is going to disturb their repose until hunger and the dropping tide decant them back onto the shore. Then the fun and games start all over again.

For the last three months I've been employed to watch shorebirds for one day per week. All bird movements have to be plotted on an hourly basis, cross-referenced against choice of feeding habitats and, of critical importance, every incidence of disturbance recorded. Then I have to distil the lot into a thudding final report. Although the pace has often been frantic, it has been an absorbing experience. In case you think I'm going soft, I won't regale you with 'A day in the life of a Bar-tailed Godwit'. Instead, here's some stuff on disturbance.

Along the shore a single road aims for a series of rock outcrops and shingle ridges but bends hard left past the army camp, taking motorists and pedestrians back from the water's edge and the roosting spots of hundreds of Oystercatchers and Dunlins. A stone's throw from where the birds roost sits Belfast City Airport which, combined with helicopters buzzing in and out of the nearby military barracks, gives the place an ambience of Saigon, circa 1974. Or, I suppose, Belfast 1994.

Yet the birds pay no attention. Drive or walk – without stopping – on the roadway and they turn a blind eye, but set one foot on the shoreline and they're off. The critical hour comes just as the tide begins to ebb. Tight packs of Turnstones and Knots emerge from their sanctuary and descend on the first exposed reefs in a feeding frenzy. They are there for around 90 minutes, by which time a wider choice of feeding places have become available; they then shift elsewhere. I have discovered that, for these species, most individuals use a limited feeding area during a particular state of the tide.

Not only are birds predictable in their daily regime, so too are people. Especially dog-walkers. It didn't take long for the pattern to form in my weekly counts. Eleven o'clock, Monday to Friday, Dastardly tales Muttley for his regular stroll along the seafront and slips him off the lead whenever he passes the army camp's gates. A salivating Muttley, his dangling tongue the colour of Rudolf's nose, rips along the beach terrorising every feathered creature in sight. If his performance coincides with an ebbing tide, then the hapless shorebirds are forced to flee to God-knows-where and won't return for hours or, in the case of Turnstones and Redshanks, not until after the next high tide.

I have no idea what dogs get out of chasing things. Once I start to think about that, I realise I don't have much idea what people get out of watching dogs chasing things either. Maybe it's nature appreciation. There's something about being out in the natural world with a purpose that makes you pay more attention to it. For bird-flushing dog owners, perhaps it's a sense of accomplishment, of dominance over lesser life forms. Doubtless there's a Darwinian explanation for this atavistic human behaviour.

Quite apart from a heartfelt sympathy for the birds, my data was being severely messed about. The thought of all the neat computer graphs being spoilt by huge gaps in the Turnstone and Redshank columns was driving me mad. I decided that the best course of action was, believe it or not, to make friends with Dastardly and hope that he would respond to subtle hints about Muttley.

I gave him a medium "Hello" – I didn't plan on us becoming bosom buddies – and got the same back. I mentioned the weather, the serenity of the open shore and finally Muttley. About the latter I said (as he playfully clawed the legs of my tripod), "He's a real bundle of life. There, there, good dog." Muttley is no big old tail-wagging Rover. No sirree. He's an airborne special forces commando terrier. Continuing with the

charade, I gave him a pet-loving stare, as if I was the breed's biggest fan. After about ten minutes of idle prattle I slipped in the crucial line: "Actually, I was trying to count the birds until Rover here flushed them all."

This ricocheted off Dastardly and came back to me as: "Well, that must have made it easier to count them. There's millions of the wee skitters hiding among the rocks." So much for diplomacy. I let matters rest for a couple more visits but was forced to rethink the softly-softly approach when Muttley's exercise programme showed no sign of slacking. I recalled the phrase: He who fails to learn the lessons of history is doomed to repeat them. Translated, this meant that tact was kaput; it was time for some guile.

One week later I was more excited than Muttley when I saw Dastardly approach. I rushed up to him, patted Muttley a few times on his Stuka-like muzzle and even restrained the brute while Dastardly read the following notice: "DANGER – UNEXPLODED ORDNANCE. During recent live fire exercises, several incendiaries overshot designated target zones and landed on the adjacent shoreline. Until these are located and defused all members of the public are strictly prohibited from leaving the public footpath. By Order. "

You may not consider this (successful) action on my part to be strictly ethical. But then, whose side are you on?

June 1997
Birdwatch

Enlightenment,
not epitaphs

I suspect that many of you will not have heard of the American Birding Association (ABA). Its membership stands at over 13,000 and it publishes *Birding*, an excellent journal. There are, regrettably, only 87 subscribers in the whole of Britain and Ireland but I happen to be one of them.

Three years ago the ABA Checklist Report for 1990 appeared in *Birding* (volume 24: 4) and featured photographs of major rarities, including a Yellow Bittern and male Narcissus Flycatcher that occurred in late May on Attu Island, Alaska.

Probably both migrants arrived after 'overshooting' their nearest breeding grounds about 1,000 miles away in Japan. They were present for more than one day, were seen by numerous observers, were easily specifically identified (a straightforward task in each case) and photographed. Then they were shot. Rather, to use the politically correct euphemism, they were 'collected'. When I discovered this I was angry. I still am. I wrote to *Birding* and questioned the justification for killing birds just because they were rarities. It is also conceivable that both birds may have been capable of reorientating to home ranges and could have bred successfully, maybe for years.

Would my protest be published? Firstly, *Birding* editor, Paul Lehman, didn't like the title – too emotive, he thought. That is precisely why I have used it again. Then he included it, not in 'Letters to the Editor', which I had intended, but in a debating forum called 'Point/Counterpoint'. Yes, I know there is such a thing as editorial prerogative, but what came next somewhat stretched the rules of fairness. My brief letter was succeeded by more than three full pages of an unashamed defence of vagrant collecting by J V Remsen Jr, from Louisiana State University's Museum of Natural Science.

So, how was something that I regard as just about indefensible, defended? It is difficult to summarize a diatribe that is much longer than a page in *Birdwatch* but among his arguments he suggested that the slaughter of birds in the Mediterranean was a more worthy cause for birders' concern than the loss of individual vagrants: "Far too many birds are dying out there for us to become emotionally involved with the deaths of a few lost, probably genetically dead, vagrants."

He even talked of a 'collecting' code of conduct and indicated some of the policies followed by collecting colleagues. For example, if someone from his university museum found a vagrant then it could be collected because: "chances are minimal that birders would be able to re-find it." Elementary, my dear Remsen! His bottom line was: "Suffice it to say that collecting for identification alone is indeed a legitimate need. Nevertheless, the vast majority of specimens of vagrants are collected not to confirm species identification, but to permit verifiable sub-species identification and to provide verifiable data on age, sex, moult, fat condition, diet and general health."

Convinced? I'm not. All birders are concerned about the loss of the planet's birdlife, but taking life needlessly breaches a moral code that doesn't have a sliding scale attached. However, let's deal with the 'science' of his arguments. Therein lies a problem. Not of possessing counter-arguments strong enough to emasculate the vagrant collecting case, but of being afforded the opportunity to state them.

Subsequent letters were received by *Birding* and two were to be published: one in support of my view, the other more pragmatic. Before they appeared I was contacted by Paul and told that Remsen was going to reply to these too – did I want a "last word" on the matter as well? I did. He received my reply promptly but, as I suspected, didn't publish it. Of course, he covered himself by being superficially even-handed for, in the end, there was no fresh rebuttal from Remsen either.

Maybe Paul thinks that this concludes the debate. Well Paul, I ask you: what didn't you like in my reply? Was it the reminder to your readership that the ABA's first rule in its Code of Ethics states: "Birders must always act in ways that do not endanger the welfare of birds"? Maybe the bit about Northern Ireland's first American

Golden Plover that was photographed, videoed and *spared* to return to its natal area on your and Remsen's continent?

However, let me repeat the part that perhaps caused greatest nuisance and was possibly shown to Remsen in order to persuade him to leave unsaid his final word so that I – in the interests of editorial impartiality, of course – could be denied mine. It is this: "Every argument which Remsen enlists (data on age, sex, moult, fat condition, general health, even genetic details) can be obtained by trapping the bird and, if needs be, taking blood, tissue and feather samples. Furthermore, *by observing the live bird,* much more information can be gained: on behaviour, species mannerisms and – importantly – voice. In fact, by killing the bird much potentially useful information is being lost, which surely makes collecting bad science."

Paul seems to lack the courage to bring this debate into the open and allow all the arguments to be heard. Perhaps his reluctance has more to do with pressure exerted by the gung-ho vested interests of American museum ornithologists.

However, like it or not, I believe that in today's world there is no justification for 'scientists' continuing to collect vagrants, which they even have the arrogance to describe as "spent genetic material." Aren't birds allowed to make occasional navigational errors on migration? Strangely enough, they possess the brains to learn from such mistakes and to rectify them. I hope that someday soon Remsen and his supporters will have the guts to rectify theirs.

May 1994
Birdwatch

"What's hit is history; what's missed is mystery." Just when we thought maxims like this had been replaced with telescopes, binoculars and brains, it seems that some 'scientists' still shoot birds to identify them.

Yes, I had fire in my belly when I wrote that. Back in 1994 my contributions to *Birdwatch* were handwritten, which made the complaint look like a covenant penned in the author's own blood. I thought, "Dominic Mitchell won't publish this". He did, despite receiving threats of litigation when he showed it in draft to Remsen. A gutsy editor, Dominic saw the article as I did. Not muckraking, not sentimental, not an ultimatum flashed by a mischievous Irish mouth. It was a manifesto born from outrage. He was not going to be brushed off by a scaremongering lawsuit. If there was ever a need for ornithological patriotism to lock horns with low-grade science, this was the time.

What has happened since? Sometimes it takes you to look back at an era to see how dead and gone it is. I don't know if some American museum 'scientists' still bag rarities. Like new president Barack Obama, I invoke the audacity of hope, and prefer to believe that such practices have been consigned to Room 101. 'Collecting' is not a favourite scab of mine that I like to scratch. So I no longer wish to sink a pick into the subject.

What of Paul Lehman? In what could have been a frosty encounter, I bumped into him at Cape May, New Jersey, shortly after the column was published. The pair of us had no time to avoid the eye contact likely to lead to a dreaded chitchat rap-crap flow of foul air. However, the notes in the conversation that followed did not chink as if struck off an icicle. Then, next day, events took an unexpected turn.

Snug in air-conditioned comfort in the front passenger seat of a luxurious people-carrier, I gazed through tinted windows as Bruce Mactavish drove. Mark Constantine and Arnoud van den Berg were in the back. It was late afternoon, we were heading south along the Garden State Parkway and approaching Cape May County. Although I'd seen it all before, the magic of wall-to-wall marshland never fades. At this time of day the dipping sun reaches an angle that shows a world of water and birds at its best. Ospreys flapped across the road, countless Laughing Gulls cruised roadside creeks and a galaxy of herons, egrets and ibises dotted the landscape as far as the eye could see. Clouds of shorebirds rose like wisps and occasionally the sky turned black as thousands fled at the approach of a Bald Eagle. I felt like John James Audubon, except I was enjoying the view from a car and not the bucking seat of a canoe.

Mark was rapt with a book that he had just bought. It was *The Birds of Cape May* by David Sibley. He started to call out the names of rarities listed in an appendix. Since Cape May is one of the 'most birded' hotspots in North America, the area's crop of once-in-a-lifetime visitors are, to a vagrant hunter, crown jewels. Among the roll-call was Wilson's Plover, a waif from southern sun-kissed beaches. Minutes later I was looking at one down the barrel of my telescope. It was among a flock of Semi-palmated Plovers. I had been engrossed by them and was playing the endless game of devil's advocate – could I tell a Semi-palmated Plover from a look-a-like Ringed Plover? – when

the Wilson's Plover swung into view. Although it was a major moment, it felt weird. It was precisely that feeling of 'the more original the discovery, the more obvious it seems afterwards.' Had serendipity played a part? Had the mention of the species just minutes before planted a seed? I will never know. However, one thing that we all knew instantly was that the bird would be big news. Just how big soon became obvious.

A few phone calls later and – faster than you could say 'breeding plumage male Narcissus Flycatcher' – Paul Lehman was at our side. He was thrilled to see the bird. It was new for his legendary list. Cars began pulling off the highway and decanting breathless birders. One driver ferreted about in the trunk and fished out a heavy object – his telescope or camera, no doubt. We didn't know who he was but Paul shot him (that is, looked in his direction) a knowing glance. "Who's that?" I asked, "Is he the guy with the gun?" Touché!

The penny dropped. He got the joke – and the point. If there is a Supreme Being, maybe he planned retribution for the death of the vagrants on Attu Island, Alaska. Collectors had shown disdain for living birds but now another vagrant would please vagrant hunters and be left alive. I have come to regard the Wilson's Plover as my gift from the Father almighty. Passed down from heaven to drive home a lesson. If the Yellow Bittern and Narcissus Flycatcher were Ghosts of Christmas Past then – I dare to hope – the Wilson's Plover might serve as a Ghost of Christmas Yet to Come. It is true what they say – what comes around, goes around.

February 2009

Faith, hope
and **ternery**

Personally, I blame God. When he was creating foxes he could have made them vegetarians. So you can't blame the red peril for being the bane of ground-nesting birds. Moreover, I suppose, there is something to be said for a furry little animal that brings out the Crocodile Dundee in a man. When it comes to foxes, I don't as much commune with nature – I lock horns with it. For wildflowers and jam, read flamethrowers and SAM (surface-to-air missile).

The nature reserve where I work – Belfast Harbour – has the scenery and rarities of the Suffolk coast but virtually no birdwatchers. Lots of things get banned. To begin with, I was banned. Before the place became a reserve nobody was allowed in, since the area encloses three military bases and all of Northern Ireland's fuel depots. The ultimate 'target-rich area'. Trespassing was obligatory. I was turfed out on a regular basis until I found a way to become a permanent resident: I got the job - poacher turned gamekeeper.

Clout that I never dreamed of possessing was an ability to ban helicopters. That came about when an embryonic tern colony in the middle of a lagoon was regularly buzzed, albeit accidentally. The joke about having Lynx, Puma and Gazelles on the reserve

wore a bit thin when the three of them were periodically frightening off the terns. I complained to the military. They declared a No-Fly-Zone and I was asked to report offenders. Gulp. "Em, but I don't want to land a pilot in bother," I said, embarrassed. "It's like this," the commander replied. "If these guys can't understand the equivalent of a big red 'No Entry' symbol on a chart then they shouldn't be flying a helicopter – this is Belfast and they are not Robert Duvall."

Unfortunately, some of them couldn't read a map. I was reluctant to pass on details – name of chopper plus serial number – until I hit upon a plan. I wanted to borrow one. The need arose after witnessing an incident on a gloomy November day. No terns were on the lagoon. They had had a successful breeding season and were now sunning themselves somewhere in Africa. All summer, electric wires around their nesting island had kept foxes at bay. So what was the fox up to that was wading out through the shallows and walking around a birdless island? Maybe it was searching for addled eggs or a tasty corpse? Nothing of the sort was out there – I had already removed all edible attractions.

What happened next threw me into a whirlwind of activity. The fox stood directly below the overhanging wires. It was looking at them. I knew it was thinking of jumping through. One leap and it would be on the island. The power had been turned off when the birds left in September. I had to move fast. I ran into a storeroom and knocked the switch back on. I felt like Frankenstein. I wanted to kebab the son-of-a-bitch, although the shock would serve only as a deterrent. It seemed to sniff out my intention and waded to a different spot. It stopped again. Then, with one Nureyev leap, it sprang upwards. A second later I was the one that had been out-foxed. It was standing on hallowed ground and looking like a prizefighter that had never had a glove laid on him. So I needed a helicopter, not as a gunship, but to rebuild the perimeter of the island.

The reason the fox got through without a shock was simple. Once its paws left contact with terra firma, it escaped being 'earthed' and the electrical circuit could not be completed. I had always assumed that a four-legged intruder would stand and touch the wire with its nose before jumping. What then, was Plan B? It was devised, not by me, but by Ivor. He said, "Phone JR, your mate in the RAF – but this time tell him that you want a helicopter hovering over the lagoon. We need it to lower telegraph poles into place. We are going to erect a poultry net right around the island – and electrify the mesh. There will be no way through that. Tell him it is payback time." "I can't say the last bit," I said, "I'll have to be nice for a change." Ivor said, "Well, whatever, use some big words like Public Elations – you are good at that sort of rigamatoosh." Ivor is a ruddy-faced farmer who helps me out with the big stuff. He is from the kawn-tree. He has hands like a baseball pitcher, a shrewd, skewed outlook on life, and a command of English that would make Roget and his thesaurus spin in the grave.

Ask him a question and he takes a deep breath before answering. What follows is likely to fizz like a Catherine wheel. One morning his child was sick. He didn't look too well himself. He reckoned he knew what the problem was. "It's all these goddamned computers people have in their houses. I don't know why folk bother with them. All you hear about is viruses. The doctor says the baby has a virus, so where do you think that came from? Answer me this: how can my wife – a fine Christian woman – go out and spend good money and come home with, not a bottle of medicine, but a box with a CD in it. She said it would sort out the bug. It was something called Mormon anti-virus. These foreign religions are on the rise you know - I don't where it will all end. Anyway, the infant's diarrhoea seems to have stopped so maybe there is something in it. You are a man of the world – what do you think?" I was tempted to exclaim, "Oh look – here comes my bus," instead I said, "Madness. The world is going mad. In the meantime, where are we going to get the telegraph poles?"

Why is it that the military have to give a day's work with a helicopter an operational title? I imagined myself as Hawkeye and Ivor as Trapper. Maybe we would be taking part in Operation Overtern? No. The airlift went under the moniker of Operation Call of Nature. Certainly, on the morning it started, part of my attire resembled incontinence pants. I was decked out like a Martian. Green waders, waterproofs and – best of all – green helmet and visor. I'm trying to think of a heroic movie actor that I might liken myself to, but I'm terrified that the inescapable resemblance was to Kermit the frog. Over previous weeks the nesting island's new frame had been assembled in an unused car park. The idea was to lay each pole horizontally and connect

"Left a bit. Hold it. Down a bit. No, back a bit. Damn. What's Harry doing up there – texting?"

up the four corners. To fit together, a sequence had to be followed.

We were determined that nothing was going to go wrong. What could go wrong? It was as simple as A, B, C and then D – follow the big white letters painted on each pole. Because the timbers had thick bases and thinner tips, there was a further consideration. Every one had to go in the right way round. To achieve that, Ivor would mark the tips. Prince Harry would have loved what happened next. The calm waters of the lagoon were transformed into a localized tsunami. The downdraft showered me and the RAF ground-controller with spray. The air turned lachrymose with aviation spirit. Communication was by hand signals. Long heavy guide ropes hung from the ends of the poles. They swayed in the air above our heads. The pilot tried repeatedly to manoeuvre the pole directly over its final resting position so that we might grab the ropes and stop it slewing around. Standing in deep mud, we could not move so had to wait for the ropes to be blown within reach. Finally I got mine. The opposite end came tantalizingly close to the ground-controller but swung away at the last minute. The pilot raised the helicopter to try and correct the pole's angle. In my determination not to lose my end of the rope I coiled it around my waist. I started to levitate!

Thoughts of having to write the longest-ever entry in the reserve accident book galvanized me into untangling myself in record time. The ground-controller started making frantic signals. I assumed that he was reminding me that RAF helicopters have right of way. Only when we had the pole in position and could remove our helmets to talk did I realise what the signalling meant. He wondered which way round the pole should be? Oh no. In the din and obscured vision neither of us had noticed Ivor's marker denoting the tip. We inspected the ends in detail, lodged for eternity in concrete moorings. The phone rang. Guess who? "Well, is she in?" It was Ivor. "Aye, she's in all right – but we didn't see your marker. The tip is facing towards Belfast but there is no marker. Is that the right direction? What did you use to mark it?" It transpired that, through pure luck, we had got it right. His marker had been a loop of masking tape that had blown away. No surprise there then. The good news was that nobody realised how close we had come to disaster. At the successful conclusion of Operation Call of Nature I shook JR's hand and commented that I now understood what the term

'military precision' meant. He laughed. Then he said, "Anthony, in 25 years of directing helicopters this is one of the few tasks that have gone without a hiccup. You boys seemed to know what you were doing – apart from the rope trick!" If only he knew.

A month later the terns were back. That was 2005. Within a couple of years their numbers grew to over 200 pairs, mainly Common Terns with some Arctic Terns. Even Roseate Terns have prospected and might yet breed. Thanks to Ivor's ingenious design no predators have got through – and they have tried. Each nesting season, the lagoon reverberates with the birds' calls. For me it is the sound of summer. I have to hear it first thing every morning from May to August so I can relax, safe in the knowledge that the night passed without mishap. I remember the two summers when I was greeted by the sound of silence. Death hung in the air. A fox had decimated the colony. Not any more. Ivor loves to visit, especially to see the chicks 'gloated' with fish and getting ready to fly. "So," he says, "is there anything else that might threaten the birds?" I said, "Not that I can think of – but you always worry about a virus."

April 2008

Reign in
Spain

Winter in the middle of the North Atlantic storm-track is a drag. Days are short, light is drab and everything is damp and cold to the touch. Heat and sunshine are a hazy dream. Constant drizzle and fog test optics and sap sanity. Only Robins defy the monotone melancholy, their fiery sunset breast a reminder of long-lost colours. In darkest January there was nothing to suggest that a change was in the air as I read down an innocent-looking fax from Ricard Gutiérrez in ultraviolet-drenched Barcelona. My reaction to what he said was to dash off a hasty instruction to the Vatican, recommending Señor Gutiérrez for canonisation: Saint Ricard, patron saint of great escapes.

On offer was a to-die-for trip to Catalonia. I could stay free in the residential quarters on the Llobregat delta reserve, bring a couple of mates and take part in the Spanish Bird Race in early May. Fantastic! Fear of performing like some dumb-ass tourist who didn't know plumage differences separating female *Sylvia* warblers, or how to tell Crested Lark from Thekla Lark on song, drove me into a frenzy of swotting over books and listening to tapes. Outside, freezing February passed into howling March, but I didn't care. I sneered at the rainfall and studied hard for my

trial alongside the impressive Barcelona front four of Gutiérrez, López, Larruy and Santaeufemia.

Logistical details were finalized in April. To save luggage space we opted for a 'beyond minimalist' approach. No sleeping bags or spare clothes were packed; just bare essentials such as sun glasses, sun-hats and insect repellent. As a reminder of things to come, the weather in Northern Ireland suddenly picked up days before we left. We interpreted this as an omen, which encouraged more stringent cutbacks. Off came all jean labels and toothbrush handles. Meeting up at the Easyjet check-in desk, I noted that John and Davy sported skinhead hair-dos to reduce bulk. For my part I'd been to the dentist and had several fillings removed. Apart from binoculars and telescopes, our combined gear for Spain would have fitted on a child's charm bracelet.

"Where are we now?" John said, sighting coast and grey-green ocean beneath a cavernous portmanteau of endless cloud. I said, "It looks like the Irish Sea but we are supposed to land at Barcelona in 15 minutes." We sat transfixed, taking in everything as the plane began its descent over a stormy Mediterranean. The surface was splattered with what appeared to be spilled yoghurt.

On closer inspection, this was the breaking crests of waves the size of credit card bills. Fishing boats hove into view, facing into the tempest yet still tossed around like eggs in a blender. As I strode through the arrivals hall in flipflops and Bermuda shorts I clocked the Yeti figure of Ricard, half-hidden but still beaming at us from underneath onion layers of thermals and Gore-tex. "I didn't know you had a winter plumage," I said. He replied, "You boys will come in handy in this weather: we could do with some help in identifying wrecked auks." He asked if we wanted to proceed with hiring a car or enquire about huskies. I said that, in keeping with the season and our frugality, we'd booked a Fiat Panda with a sunroof but no heater.

It's a short drive from Barcelona airport to Llobregat delta reserve. It ought to be: the airport is built over part of the reserve. Other chunks of the habitat are also gone for good from what was once an intertwined wetland where Mother Nature soaked up a river system and fed a much larger area with life. The loss of marshland is a familiar story in people-packed Europe and I'll leave you to brood about that on your own. In the meantime, Ricard and his band of brothers have rescued the best bits and now he was tending to another pressing task, which was pointing out the locations of speed cameras on the dual carriageway leading past the reserve's entrance. Ricard commented, "'We should twin your reserve at Belfast with this one – they have a lot in common." Up to a point he was right. Both are on the edge of a city that begins with 'B'. After that, all comparisons were downhill.

Ensconced in a majestic timber viewpoint, we contemplated a scene redolent of Ancient Egyptian tomb engravings that I remembered from childhood. Egrets and Black-winged Stilts danced in the shallows, Garganey slumbered among wet tussocks and swarms of martins, swallows and swifts bustled back and forth below a threatening firmament. Audouin's Gulls driven inland from wave-lashed beaches mingled with Avocets and Mediterranean Gulls. Above them Whiskered, Black and White-winged Black Terns dipped and fluttered like windborne pages of burnt newspaper. Cameo performances came thick and fast. Little Bitterns burst into flight from clumps of reeds, their black and gold upperparts flashing like a matador's cape. Then, distant rumbling. Not thunder but a faint cacophony recalling the yelp of migrating geese. The source could be picked out as strange twig-like formations suggesting coat hangers in the sky. Line after line crystallized from the heavens and then dropped in long rippling rows, manoeuvring into the stiff wind with a dexterity surprising for creatures built like skeletons. 'Good grief' I said, 'I've never seen such a mass break-out of Greater Flamingos in my life.' The presumed escapees (years of British and Irish brainwashing are hard to shake off) were unfazed by the weather conditions, which is more than could be said about us. That night we huddled for warmth in front of an open fridge and plotted a dash to the Ebro delta next morning in an attempt to get into the lee of the rain front saturating the western Mediterranean from Sardinia to the Pyrenees.

The plan backfired. The centre of the depression slipped southwards and caught us amidships. At L'Ametella de Mar, language problems seemed insuperable in a supermarket until the serving lady came out from behind the counter and did the shopping for us. She topped the trolley off with three large plastic bags and pointed to our heads. "Do you think she knows about the leaky roof in the car?" John said. "No, I reckon we just look destitute," I replied. The Ebro delta is as flat as Cliff Richard lyrics and juts out into the sea like a big sore thumb. Irrigated fields are ubiquitous, among which a latticework of small roads leads to gigantic lagoons packed with birds. At least that is the theory. 'Before driving across the delta be sure to obtain a detailed map.' We missed this piece of small print but it didn't appear to matter. Everywhere we saw pairs of Kentish Plovers – male invariably on the right, presumably the lee side – standing on mud banks dividing flooded rice paddies. After an hour, estimates for the number of pairs varied widely. John and I calculated at least 100, whereas Davy, who was trying his best to navigate through wipers and using a map the size of a beer mat, felt that we had only seen one – repeatedly. Gradually the realization dawned that the Bangladesh feel to the landscape wasn't entirely normal. The whole place was inundated and sopping wet, with some roads barely above water level. After the deluge, the delta's farmland offered birds no more refuge than the open sea, except for isolated patches of marginally higher ground.

Slowly and miraculously two days of incessant downpour eased to a pattering rain and then ceased. Free at last to walk around, we discovered what the weather had done. A river of migrants heading north to destinations from France to the Arctic Circle had been grounded. Europe's birds were at our feet. Eight kinds of warbler hopped underneath a bush the size of a snooker table, along with three species whose names soon became a mantra: Pied Flycatcher, Redstart, Whinchat. We saw Pied Flycatchers in window boxes, on bicycles, inside bus shelters and in green plastic trees at beach bars. Birds that had been unable to feed were weak and tame. A muddy vegetable allotment held 26 Collared Pratincoles at arm's length. All revved-up to breed, each defended a tiny territory and ignored us completely. In the strange blue light, their red bill bases

sparkled like lipstick and breast plumage had the tawny glow of a single malt whisky. Picking, probing and darting between them moved a hyperactive horde. There were Temminck's and Little Stints, Wood Sandpipers and Short-toed Larks, a kaleidoscope of yellow wagtail heads and, best of all, a roaring Red-throated Pipit.

Business beckoned. Memories of Ebro were canned – a male Red-footed Falcon hunting from telegraph wires, side-by-side views of Icterine and Melodious Warblers, clouds of shorebirds – and we returned to Barcelona. John and Davy, both non-combatants in the event, left for Aiguamolls de l'Empordá where, mirabile dictu, they found an American Golden Plover next day. I donned a green shirt, strapped on the shin guards and cleaned my lenses for Ireland. Captain Fantastic and his Catalan compatriots had prepared a killer itinerary not only for the bird race but also an attempt on the Spanish day list record of 169. I too was ready. I didn't tell them at the time, but I was planning to follow Dutch taxonomic rules so I could count even more species than they did: ensuring an Irish birding victory over Spain. Before we plunged into the Costa del Darkness, we consulted the Internet to get the latest meteorological projection for the next 24 hours. A deep area of low pressure was steaming into our path. Its estimated amount of precipitation was so large that the satellite imagery contained a written warning: 'Unless your name is Noah, do not travel tomorrow.'

We took the chequered flag in pitch darkness high on a mountainside scented with the Mediterranean night. A dog barked and a jet droned high overhead. Nothing. Not even a cicada. Maybe the birds had heard the forecast as well? Feeble at first and then rising and falling in the breeze, a Nightjar broke

Here is a special postcard from Spain for Mrs McGeehan. Just some of the bird riches to be seen in Catalonia – even in the course of one day!

our duck. A Nightingale woke up in the ravine below and then the first real scalp fell – an Eagle Owl chick began begging audibly for food. Other nocturnal rendezvous yielded Scops Owl, Barn Owl and Little Owl, but Long-eared Owl, Tengmalm's Owl and Red-necked Nightjar remained stubbornly tight-lipped. Sleepwalking Little Ringed Plovers were identified by silhouette in a roadside pool and restless marsh birds squawked and crooned their way on to the score sheet. Spirits lifted as we sped towards the Pyrenees. Then it started raining, not birds, but cats and dogs. The last hour of the night ought to have been a birdsong bonanza; instead it turned into a wash-out. At dawn we should have surveyed a vista straight out of The Sound of Music. Alas, mists were down, valleys were wrapped in fog and all roads leading up to subalpine slopes were blocked with falling snow.

Were we downhearted? Not in the slightest. One of the secrets for amassing a respectable tally is to spin thin chances into whole cloth. In the murky conditions we couldn't see Ring Ouzel, Black Redstart and Water Pipit but we could recognize them by sound. Or, rather, my teammates could. As we zigzagged down through a succession of habitats, the cross hairs of eyes and ears tuned to the sensitivity of hair triggers plucked species out of tree canopy, scrub and sky. The pace was electric. We stuck to the list manager's tight schedule, which meant that one bird-rich vein had to be vacated for another by a deadline that was unshakeable: "Two minutes to get Dipper, Grey Wagtail, Bullfinch and Song Thrush." The team rallied and produced a series of last-gasp tackles on a par with Roy Keane at his most glorious. By lunchtime we were back at Llobregat. I got a feeling that it was payback time for the delta's birds. If they didn't show up and be counted, Ricard would send in the avaricious evil of developers next week. They showed up. Not one but seven Great Spotted

Cuckoos sat together on the airport's fence, a Montagu's Harrier flopped past, a Purple Gallinule came out after weeks spent undercover, and a lone Red-rumped Swallow reported for duty among ranks of hirundines that numbered thousands.

Even the weather cut us an ace. The rain stopped and a cool east wind blew seabirds inshore as if it was September, not May. Gannet and Shag were quickly in the bag. Right then it happened – the ornithological domino effect. A Little Tern led to a Gull-billed Tern; a flock of Balearic Shearwaters attracted a trio of Arctic Skuas; a squadron of incoming shearwater shapes metamorphosed into a posse of 16 Pomarine Skuas – flanked by two European Storm Petrels. Onward. The light and our luck held. Coastal maquis and mesquite were blitzed for Dartford Warbler and shrikes, crumbling cliffs scanned for Black Wheatear and Blue Rock Thrush. The day ended in triumph. At dusk we hit 173 species. Our last bird was a roosting Red-billed Waxbill – an accidental human introduction that has gone bush – so we counted it. We weren't fussy by that stage. Ricard started throwing around big fatherly hugs like a Spanish Mick McCarthy; I finally got to finish breakfast.

Not usually a compulsive shopper, Davy disappeared into the duty-free mall at Barcelona airport as John and I waited to board the plane home. He returned with an air of celebration, jangling three bottles that he distributed, one apiece. 'What's this?' we asked, expecting to sample a rare vintage. "It's fake tan," he said, "I don't know about you two but I'm not going back to work looking like I spent ten days in the rain!"

August 2002
Dutch Birding

Sun, sea ...
and **him**

On holiday with a tripod **by Mrs McGeehan**

Dear reader, this is being written in the departure lounge at Palma airport at the end of a family holiday. The kids said to say hello. I've no message from their father. He's over at the window – 'scoping flocks of swifts – in the vain hope of finding an elusive Pallid Swift in the dying moments of the 'trip' (one of his many Freudian slips this week).

Well I suppose I've had a pretty good time considering the problems with the hotel and the weather. We stayed at the Alcudia Pins, which seemed perfect in the brochure. Right on the beach, nice pool and quiet – well away from the nightlife.

It wasn't until we arrived that I discovered the reason for this isolation: the Albufera marsh was all around us. He was jubilant. He said, "You've certainly scored three lemons picking this place." Right there and then I sure felt like one.

For April the weather was mostly fine: sunny and dry during the day but very cold at night. There was no heat in the rooms and not enough bedclothes, which turned his male heir into a bed-wetter. Not that he noticed. He was up and out for dawn every morning, arriving back via the beach for a poolside breakfast about 11 o'clock. By the middle of the week even the other hotel guests could set their watches by him (although by then they looked away out of politeness).

You couldn't miss him: staggering across the sand, picking his way through the bikinis, laden down with optics and *getting paler* by the day. One morning a kindly big German lady spotted him and asked me what he did. I told her he was an 'orno-addict' but I think she got the wrong idea. She sunbathed on her balcony after that.

Physically, I saw a lot more of my husband than expected, but mentally he was usually somewhere else. Take our conversation while out for a stroll.
"Anthony, there's a barbecue at the hotel tonight."
"Hoopoe calling."
"I'd like to go to it."
"Osprey overhead."
"I think the kids would enjoy it."
"Wow! Audouin's Gull on the beach. Must dash and get the camera."
"ANTHONY! You never listen. I said there's a barbecue at the hotel tonight."
"Hey kids – want to go to a barbie tonight?"

"YEAH! Brilliant dad."

"Okay. Mum will tell you about it. I'll be back in a minute."

Grrr – see what I mean?

One useful discovery I made came as a result of noticing what he records in his notebook. For days he had been bleating about not finding any Pallid Swifts, which were his "number one target for the holiday." I sympathized. Twice I let him disappear for the afternoon in pursuit of this seemingly mythical quarry. He 'dipped' each time.

Later in the apartment he was having difficulty tracing a swift silhouette out of a field guide so I held down the page for him. Then I read the following: "18 April. North edge of Albufera. Excellent views of two Pallid Swifts in evening light. Got all features including 'hoary' head pattern and blunt wing tips." And, for 19 April: "Perfect looks at several Pallids, even better than yesterday."

For the moment I'm saying nothing about detecting this latest ruse – except to tell you that I've started a little notebook of my own. I've entitled it 'Exhibit A'.

Midweek witnessed a charm offensive. A surprise bottle of champagne, perfume (*Chanson de Nuit* – you can guess why he picked that) and breakfast in bed, all designed to confuse me. He took the kids out bike-riding all day and left me in peace by the pool with a large G&T and a good book. Nuts to work, debt and wiping runny noses. Tucked inside the pages of the book (*A Woman in Your Own Right* by Anne Dickson, read it sometime) I found an old postcard, one he sent from Sri Lanka. I'll just read you part of it: "Had an incredible morning. Trekked

through cloud forest to the edge of a mountain plateau. Arrived at a place called World's End and sat and watched the mist clear. Breathtaking scenery. Thought lots about you and took many pictures. It is heaven out here but I still cannot wait to get home. Hugs and kisses."

I thought to myself, yes, he really has a normal side after all. By seven o'clock I was even starting to miss him. Then he arrived with the news that he'd found a nice restaurant for dinner. We had a lovely meal, *al fresco* even. As we finished, the rays of a Mediterranean sunset cast a golden glow on our faces. A perfect photo opportunity. He reached for the camera and – click – took a hasty shot of the kids (with their faces still caked in Bolognese sauce).

I asked him, "Aren't you going to take any pictures of me?" Spontaneously, and without the faintest sound of a penny dropping, he replied: "No, I was only finishing off the roll with my Audouin's Gull shots on it." If I'd had a dictionary handy I would have clobbered him with it and then told him to look up words such as 'tact', 'thoughtfulness' and 'chauvinist'. Instead, I tried some satire. "You didn't happen to take 35 of them by any chance?" "More like 71," he replied.

All of which reminds me of an advertisement I once saw that I could easily have placed. It read, "For sale: one man. Little used, would suit spare room, deep pile on underside." Actually, it didn't say 'man'. It said 'mat' – just my little Freudian slip.

"Last call for flight … " Time to go. I'd better retrieve him from his perch at the window. I suppose I'll stick with him, even though

He was pretty sick when he saw this snap. I said, "What's the big deal, it's just a sea-gull. There were lots of them on the beach that day. Now, let me think, where were you at the time?"

I don't like him very much right now. Of course, he'll probably be considerate and nice to me – having managed to bag a Pallid Swift in the nick of time before take-off. Phew! Wasn't *that* lucky? Just wait until he gets home.

November 1994
Birdwatch

Douze Pointes
Lark

Dupont's Lark. Dupont was French and the French make lovely names. How did you pronounce the surname? Did you say "Dew-punt," or employ some savoir-faire and give it a bit of Gallic wellie by making a 'Dew-bon' sound but transpose the 'bon' into 'pon'? If you speak the word while looking into a mirror, you end up with your lips in a circle and your mouth open. You look like a mullet. Moreover, you know what the French do to mullets – they eat them. That is what you get for putting on continental airs and graces. Yes, to save public ridicule we are lumbered with the rough, gruff, hard terminal 't'.

What does Dupont mean? Crudely translated, it means dweller by the bridge. The word's origin is from the Latin 'pons' meaning bridge, which became 'pont' in Old French. Humdrum? Never. Stick a French moniker in front of a bird's name and the result is a messianic title guaranteed to set your emotions ablaze. Audouin, Jouanin, Ménétries, Verreaux. Amazingly, all four were Parisians, whose trails stretched far and wide – but mainly southwards. Thank God they weren't English. Boring plebeian names such as Baker, Potter, Plumber or Hopwood would have clung like a bad smell and tainted the species. Irish eponyms

would have been worse. A reminder of Sunday mass. The priest reads out the list of the faithful departed, his Adam's apple slowly rising and falling in time with a pulpit-timed cadence: Brigid O'Malley, Patrick Casey, Eamon Fitzwalter.

Let me introduce you to one of the great laws of bird names. Where a species bears the name of a person, a good story is attached. Sacrilege is committed when commemorations are changed. White-rumped Sandpiper used to be called Bonaparte's Sandpiper, consigning Charles Lucien Jules Laurent Bonaparte – younger brother of Napoleon – and his connection with the species to Room 101. In North America, Oldsquaw was recently changed to Long-tailed Duck for reasons of political correctness. That is like taking Jesus off the crucifix and replacing him with Santa Claus.

Who was Monsieur Dupont and how did he find Europe's shyest bird? The plot thickens when you realise that the species occurs, not in France, but in the deserts of North Africa and parts of Spain. Such questions create great pools of imagination where it is possible to sit and dream of how things might have happened.

The moon set and the sun rose, each marking the passage of time during which Magnus stood motionless, listening. Like a fool I enquired, "Say, Magnus, I don't suppose there's a handy place for breakfast in this neck of the woods (I mean desert)?"

Dupont was probably part of a nineteenth century generation of French ornithologists who rushed like a flood across North Africa collecting specimens and hoping to stumble into a personal holy grail – a bird new to science. I invoke a vision of desert landscapes, camel trains and dusk encampments around crackling campfires under a million stars. Conversation is in French, of course. However, if the scene was subtitled, the line 'Guys, nothing beats this,' is bound to have been used.

Sorry to disappoint, but a Foreign Legionnaire he was not. Leonard Puech Dupont was born at Bayeux, in Normandy, in 1795. He became so well known in French natural history circles that when Louis Vieillot described a new species of lark in 1820 based on a specimen collected in Provence and tagged with the single word 'Dupont', Vieillot assumed that the initials 'LP' had been omitted purely because they were superfluous. That would be tantamount to wondering if there was more than one railway engineer called Brunel.

In 1817, Dupont was hired by Joseph Ritchie, Private Secretary to the British Ambassador in Paris, to accompany him on a journey penetrating across the Sahara to search for the source of the Niger. Dupont's role was to assist 'for the purpose of collecting and preparing objects of natural history'. Sadly, the expedition had a tragic end. Crossing Libya, Ritchie died in the Sahara at Murzuk, 450 miles south of Tripoli. Dupont's movements are unknown since he resigned from the expedition before it left Tripoli! Nevertheless, by 1819 he was back in Paris, bristling with a large collection of birds, reptiles and insects. Perhaps, when Vieillot chanced upon the specimen that became *Chersophilus duponti*, it had been

among the booty from North Africa, rather than hailing from Provence – where the lark is unknown today.

However, the specimen's French connection cannot be dismissed lightly. Vieillot clearly stated that the individual he described had been found in Provence. Leonard Dupont died just eight years later, oblivious to the confusion that still reigns. Even in death his was not the final denouement, which occurred in 1873. In that year a different Monsieur Dupont passed away, aged 75. He too had been a Parisian natural history dealer and his name is honoured in *Tilmatura dupontii*, Dupont's Hummingbird, no less. Do we have our man? Well, sort of. In a nutshell, Europe's rarest lark is certainly named after a bloke called, for short, Dupont.

With the exception of a spring lamb gambolling into a slaughterhouse, there is nothing in the natural world as foredoomed as the chances of clapping eyes on a Dupont's Lark. This is not because the bird is on the brink of extinction. The reason is its secretive habits, which rival those of Osama bin Laden. The species is a runner, not a flyer. Its habitat is rolling prairie. Steppe grassland or plains of tussocky vegetation are its home. It is out there – on the range, among the crickets.

I tried to nail one in 2003, at a breeding site in Catalonia. The Spanish researcher driving the Landrover had just finished telling me that we had no chance of seeing the species – but we might hear the song – when one popped out and stood for 20 minutes on a bare patch between low shrubs. It was a freak event. He was speechless, yet I wasn't surprised. It was evening and the sun was dipping and turning the new grass gold. The sky was full of sound. A galaxy of larks was aloft. In truth, it

Spanish steppe, nature's magic carpet. Sadly, note the ploughed-up strips in the background: like a whiff of urine in paradise.

was dozens of one-man bands, each a Calandra Lark. I wasn't surprised at my luck because it came at the end of a perfect day. From dawn we had toured the last remaining patches of virgin Catalonian steppe. Everywhere we went we saw sights that are vanishing. The birds – bustards, sandgrouse, raptors – were amazing but the news was heartbreaking. The steppe is going under the plough to produce fruit for which there is no market or need. Destroying steppe is a vote-catcher, however. All day I felt as though the birds were performing for me. Unexpectedly revealing themselves like a deeply worried rainforest tribe who see their world trashed and are desperately beseeching a stranger to help.

In Aragón province the situation is less grim, but here too it feels like a sword of Damocles is poised to strike. There is, however, a steppe reserve. Compared to the majesty of the surrounding landscape – canyons and buttresses above which drift columns of vultures – it is pitifully small. And, if you believe 'the gen', it is a nap location for seeing Dupont's Larks. You mean by tape-luring a bird into view? Magnus Robb, Pim Wolf and I were never going to do that. In fact, I had already reconciled myself to the fact that I was probably not going to see one. Oddly enough, that didn't bother me. On the other hand, it would be a major league disappointment not to hear the song, which Magnus was here to record. Here, so you know what to expect, is part of what *Birds of the Western Palearctic* says about vocalisations: 'Song resembles twittering of Linnet.' Really? We'll see about that.

Out here in the Celtic fringe, there is a popular little word. That word is thrawn. It signifies obstinacy, cussedness, or just plain exasperating. If you are thrawn you are not cooperating. Even when singing, Dupont's Lark is thrawn. For one thing, it sings mainly in the still of the night. If, at daybreak, you try to track down the little chanter, it falls silent and sneaks away. Then, if it feels like singing some more, it takes itself off to the heavens where you cannot see it. Up there, it moves around and the song bursts are so short that you don't have enough time to get a bead on the songster's dizzy location. On windy days or nights – fairly typical steppe weather - it does not sing at all. There is no such thing as a shoo-in Dupont's Lark!

In a bid to out-smart the species we devised a plan. We were confident that we had discovered its Achilles' heel, a flaw in its evasion tactics. The strategy was simple. It was called a night attack. At dusk we drove to a survey plot and walked and walked. Ordinarily, the sound of Little Owls barking under a hunter's moon would be memorable. That night they did nothing for me. I was cold, tired, and larkless. We all were. It was early February. We knew the birds sang a lot in late February. Maybe we were two weeks too early? One thing we couldn't complain about was the weather. It was perfect. It was calm and icy cold with night frosts so there wasn't a breath of wind during the two hours before dawn.

We decided to bite the bullet. Although a long haul, we upped sticks and drove to the steppe reserve near Belchite, in Aragón. In the faint starlight there seemed to be nothing to see; no fences, no trees or hills, no streamlines or fields. There was nothing but slightly undulating land and we were on the only road. I had the feeling that we had reached the edge of a different world, outside man's jurisdiction. "Maybe, if we drive around in the dark, we might hear one from the comfort of the car," I said, wistfully. I was half right. Magnus heard it first and

was out of the car like a rocket. He was on autopilot. In pitch-blackness he frantically unfurled a mess of cables and stuck more leads into more monitors that an episode of ER. In short order the three of us dressed for the performance. We were in full Amundsen kit. We should, perhaps, have donned tuxedos. The sound was mesmerizing. It came in echoing gasps, as if vainly using a bicycle pump to inflate a hovercraft. Each lazy stanza hung in the night air and evaporated. I sat down among beards of frost on clumps of vegetation and watched Magnus slowly get closer to the singer. His breath rose like steam in the biting cold. Now was the time to be really, really quiet. Hearing the solo performance cleared up a few things. Dupont's Lark is a diva. Its notes are as fragile as eggshell and require complete hush to avoid being drowned out.

It was a long sit. The sun came up and started to get the cold out of my bones. The morning sky turned an indescribable blue, bright and cloudless, hard as enamel. The air began to fill with the sound of other larks. Five species in total. Many Lesser Short-toed Larks clawed the air. You could see them easily, no bother. They were singing straight at the sun, heads thrown back, chests a-quiver. We stayed out all day in the sun, Magnus making painstaking recordings. Pim was the only person to see a Dupont's Lark. I fell asleep when a nimble breeze blew warm sweet gusts and woke with that blissful feeling of strange surroundings obliterating a recollection of where you were when you nodded off. I said to Pim, "This place is so peaceful, it is like going back in time." "Oui," he replied, "Y'a rien de plus beau les amis." Precisely. Now, where did I hear that before?

March 2008

Letter from
America

Mark Constantine, without whom none of this would have happened, usually nods off over the Greenland ice cap. He would never admit to it, but coming so close to the North Pole, I know that he doesn't like to look. It is not so much connected to his fear of edges and belief in a flat Earth; I suspect it has more to do with Santa Claus and not wanting to gaze down and discover no trace of a team of Reindeer in these parts. Mark is good at keeping dreams alive and despite his snores and annexation of my armrest, he has left me in peace to wonder what might be living in the snowy landscape thirty thousand feet below us.

I love this Icelandair flight and these trips to New Jersey. It is a long day that starts in London and ends with a touchdown on a spring evening at JFK in New York. We meet Bruce Mactavish, just arrived from Newfoundland where it is still winter. In the airport parking lot, I hear Laughing Gulls and scent flowers; Bruce whiffs spilled beer on patio tables and barbecue smells wafting on balmy air. For him, this is Copacabana. Although body clocks are ready for bed, the sun is still to set. Across the Big Apple people are just knocking off work. On our journey northwest, Manhattan punches the skyline and the Verrazano-Narrows Bridge carries us high across the wide tidal waters marking the entrance to the Hudson. The tops of the mile-long suspension bridge tower overhead. They are so high that, unless you are seated in a convertible, you cannot crane your head back far enough to see where they finish. Multiple lanes of oncoming traffic snake over the bridge, many turning on headlights whose single brilliances transform the scene into one of Lilliputian grandeur. The bridge becomes a vast candlelit procession and we are part of it. North America shrinks you and makes you feel like a nickel tossed into the Grand Canyon. It is a good experience, a mental shampoo.

Along with Arnoud van den Berg, we are a team taking part in the World Series of Birding. The four of us have a week to prepare a route stitching together the richest bird habitats within the state of New Jersey. If scouting goes well, come race day, we will record at least 200 species in 24 hours. Bayshore, swamp, pine barrens and cedar bogs, sloughs and swales – American habitats come in many forms and with their own names. To begin with, we will be in the top left-hand corner of the state, a land of sylvan everything. The state line is meaningless. An hour's drive west of New York the countryside

Nobody is better at pulling the birds than Bruce 'McSpish' Mactavish.

81

starts to rise. The twisted and folded Kittatinny Mountains link western New Jersey with Georgia hundreds of miles to the south, and stretch as a great cat's-paw of forested highlands north into Canada. Broadleaved forest is continuous and migrating Broad-winged Hawks follow the leafy ridgelines for thousands of miles. In 1826 James Fenimore Cooper wrote *The Last of the Mohicans*, a swashbuckling tale based on events that unfolded in these very mountains, rivers and valleys. Most of the habitats are still intact. I will let his words set the scene, "It was a feature peculiar to the colonial wars of North America that the toils and dangers of the wilderness were to be encountered before the adverse hosts could meet. Armies larger than those that had disposed of whole countries were seen to bury themselves in these forests, whence they rarely returned, except in skeleton bands."

We stayed in the only accommodation for miles around. Plain wooden cabins with feeders out front attracted a blizzard of small birds. Dead Big Game was on show behind the reception desk. Turkey beards and deer heads hung on the walls; a bearskin rug covered the floorboards beside a rocking chair. If Wild Bill Hiccock had appeared nobody would have been surprised. I expected to scoff at anything from the roly-poly locals with fuzzy beards and oil-stained dungarees to the blueberry pancakes with enough cream on the side to build an igloo. Instead, I was converted. I was converted to the easy camaraderie and slow-paced inquisitiveness of the people. And I was pleased that they loved America, blessed it, and cherished its wildness. Sure, we did see Turkey-hunters but they were friendly and wedded to the woods. Occasionally we glimpsed their quarry – not moving a muscle, stock-still, holding themselves in frozen symmetry with dappled

surroundings. Apart from aircraft rumbles high overhead, the only sounds rattling our brains came from the forest. "What's that?" I said. "A Black Bear," said Arnoud, who heard the same *mmmumph* from not far away. He imitated the sound. The bear answered! Mark, who was a short distance ahead of us, beat a hasty retreat. We passed him – going the other way. Arnoud tried once more. Again the bear answered. Now we could see it. It shot us a dismissive look and lumbered off, its footfalls silent as the big recumbent silhouette rose and melted away among a livery of fresh green leaves.

Time to take the big examination. All winter I had been practicing North American birdsong identification by listening to CDs while driving to work, vacuuming the house and doing the ironing. Then, when I went down with housemaid's knee, I listened to them in bed. North American birders are different to many of us. When you tap them for knowledge they like to make sure that you 'get it'. They communicate to share, not to impress. Dick Walton's *Birding by Ear* became my bible. His voice and avuncular manner was Disney to my ears. One tip was to invent a mnemonic for each sound. Yanks call them handles. Rather than try and remember the sound itself, the trick is to remember the handle. The system relies on finding an unforgettable aide-memoire, which cements the sound into your consciousness. Analogies are personal – "If it works for you," Bruce would say. Mark found the concept Freudian. That was my fault for telling him a few of my innermost mnemonics. Sora: the noise made in an empty house by an unauthorized person; Blackpoll Warbler: the hiss of a sewage farm sprinkler; Ruffed Grouse: the sound of inflating a sheep's stomach with a bicycle pump; Bobolink flight call: a fairy's fart.

I couldn't come up with a prompt for Hermit Thrush. Maybe, if we heard one in life, I might find a reason to remember it – sometimes place and time can affix a sound forever. We got directions to a high escarpment where winter still held sway. New leaves, as yet unfurled, clustered thick along ashen bark. Melted snow had filled streams to overflowing and created cool vapours where waters cold as Saturn plunged into ravines and became white-water rapids. In contrast to the greenery of numberless trees on the lower slopes, this was a fastness of stunted boughs and quiet solemnity. A Pileated Woodpecker broke the silence with sonorous ack-ack gun drumming. Somewhere in the distance a smaller woodpecker made a few lazy taps. It began to rain. Heavy drops pitter-pattered on dead leaves and the sky turned the colour of a tin roof.

"I hear it," Bruce said. Movement ceased and we all strained to listen. The notes were thin and somewhat wiry, yet also desolate and delicate. We moved closer. The rain eased but the sky darkened. Peels of thunder rang out. The atmosphere acquired an eve of destruction heaviness. Like a file of stalking Mohicans, we slunk silently around boulders and ducked under brittle branches. Soon we were within the soloist's ken. We stopped short of its song-post among a tracery of twigs that resembled tendrils of petrified chewing gum. It was aware of us but decided to treat us like tiptoeing latecomers to a performance and continued regardless, a little gall of a bird with a kind eye and rusty tail. The Hermit Thrush thought it was singing to attract a mate, but it made a permanent work of art in my head: the decaying damp of mossy logs, the dignity of living trees, an expectation of lightning about to strike. I refuse to succumb to euphemisms

The singer hid his face deep in the shadows. In fact, it was better to listen, not look.

to describe what we heard. It was such a song that, when the bird stopped singing, you felt like whispering Amen.

April 2008

The
big one

Sometimes I run out of kind words to say. I am not a journalist who goes around the world poking his nose into trouble spots and digging for tragedy and strife. Nor do I want to gain penetrating insights, discover deep truths or grasp the socio-economic reasons preventing the import of Cuban cigars into the USA. All I want is to tiptoe away from humanity and watch birds in peace. But does this happen? I first ventured east of the Isle of Man in 1977. Being Irish I decided to snub England and hit my first foreign avifauna at Calais – a Crested Lark. From here I zipped around Europe by train, chaperoned by a bunch of student confrères who were smarter than me. They were not remotely interested in birds but I needed them because they could decipher the baffling train timetables. I saw Whiskered Terns hawking over Venetian canals, scored Alpine Swift above Mount Etna and 'pished' Firecrest and Short-toed Treecreeper in the grounds of the Vatican – the others were inside at the time gawking at a few hand-painted ceilings.

Maybe this blasphemous act outraged Saint Peter and the gang since, after Rome, the trip went pear-shaped. That night, sleeping in the passageway of an overnight train to Belgrade, I was booted awake by a Yugoslav border guard. I woke up looking down the barrel of a gun. The hole where the bullet comes out looked surprisingly small, yet what a big difference it would make to my chances of seeing Blue Rock Thrush on the Acropolis. Imminent danger receded a little when the bozo scratched his ear with the gun sight on the muzzle. Then, as far as I could tell, the insults started. He looked down on me with a derisory Hannibal Lecter leer and snapped, "Pisspot." Remembering what you are supposed to do when rumbled by a sullen bear, I curled up, made myself as small as possible, and played dead for my life's worth. It was no good. "Pisspot, pisspot, pisspot!" Oh dear. I squirmed around the floor, employing as many worried hand gestures as possible and was relieved when he seemed to reciprocate. Why, he even held out his big mitt. I was about to grab it when the truth dawned. This wasn't the hand of friendship; all he wanted was to check my passport. I never thought I could have wound up arrested on account of incorrect comprehension of English, but it was close.

In May 2001 lightning struck twice. The World Series of Birding is a 24-hour bird race held within the borders of the state of New Jersey. It's birdwatching Jim, but not as we know it. However,

"This one's for you, Art. Speaking personally, give me a dicky-bird every time."

85

the borderline insanity of attempting to amass a species tally in excess of 200 in a single day is more than offset by the money raised for bird and habitat conservation. In recent years this has exceeded $250 000. It's a long story, but I usually get to take part – provided US immigration control officials let me in. Why wouldn't they? The red tape started on the plane. The American air-hostess asked what nationality I was. "Irish," I said. "Okay – you are EC." So much for a cultural heritage spanning two millennia. Becoming European at a stroke obliged me to fill in a Non-immigrant Visa Waiver Arrival Form. At the top it said, 'Welcome to the USA'. Then the gloves came off. 'Have you ever been or are you now involved in espionage or sabotage; or in terrorist activities; or genocide; or between 1933 and 1945 were you involved, in any way, in persecutions associated with Nazi Germany or its allies?' Faced with questions like that, it is easy to understand why some sections of the British public want to opt out of Europe.

I had a bigger problem with the next enquiry. 'Are you a person of moral turpitude?' Somehow I find it hard to associate morals with anything originating from across the pond, although this overlooks the contribution of McDonalds. Specifically, the 'green' recyclable quality of their food, which has given succour to vagrant Laughing Gulls in restaurant car-parks at Groningen, the Netherlands, and Coleraine, Northern Ireland. So I ticked the box. Funny word, 'turpitude'. I have to confess that I hadn't come across it before. Nevertheless, juxtapositioned with 'moral' it is bound to mean something vaguely similar – maybe 'fibre', 'standing' or even 'certitude'? Wrong. Little did I know it, but I'd just crossed swords with one of the most dangerous terms on the planet. This nine-letter noun got me hauled out of the customs queue and interrogated by an attack hamster

with more braid on his uniform than Idi Amin. Turpitude, in case you don't know, means baseness, depravity or vileness. I got a grilling but my newfound citizenship came to the rescue and spared deportation. Being a European ignoramus I couldn't possibly have known what the question meant. Vive la différence!

One thing I love about America is its wildness, a quality that is reflected in its citizens. Unlike Europeans, Yanks don't sit relaxed outdoors sipping tiny cups of coffee; instead they hang around indoors in air-cooled comfort drinking 20-ounce schoonerfuls of the stuff. This, I suppose, is to keep them awake and ready to defend their country. They are armed and waiting. Turn off remarkably litter-free highways just a few hours south of New York and you snake through beautiful unspoiled backcountry. At a spot called Dividing Creek a cracked two-lane rural road skirts salt marshes the size of Luxembourg. Swaying forest fringes a morass of channels and you pass occasional beat-up shrimp boats tied to rickety docks. The few houses are on stilts. This is Bald Eagle country. Also, in the minds of the locals, it might still harbour a few lurking Vietcong. We were spotted by a one-man scouting patrol. A cloud of dust marked his approach.

"What the hell are you guys doing?" The driver appeared to use the same tailor as Johnny Rotten and had a face made for radio. In the heat, two strands of hair were melted to his head and his beer belly luxuriated over the steering wheel. In my reply I decided to put eagles first and other birds firmly last. Except for Turkeys – I guessed he liked to hunt them. In the rear of his pick-up he had a double-barrelled pump-action shotgun. "Neat gun," I said. He and I started to get along fine after that remark. He introduced himself as Art and tried to be helpful. Despite being almost within sight of an occupied eyrie we were, according to him, in completely the wrong place. "Why, I see whole flocks over my farm." With that he left, but not for long. Minutes later he was back. He'd found two soaring eagles. We jumped into our vehicle and disappeared into the sandstorm boiling up in his wake. We anticipated a misidentification – most likely the birds were Turkey Vultures. If so, what should we do about it? Telling him he was wrong could have fatal consequences. He pointed frantically upwards and we baled out of the car. The birds were about to disappear over woods, so I had to be quick. However, the single look was a good one. More than long enough to see that they were Red-tailed Hawks. "Did you see 'em?" he pleaded. I chickened out. "Sorry Art, they drifted off just as I got on them." I slipped in a few swear words to sound macho and for safety's sake. We said cheerio again but, foolishly, didn't make a bolt for freedom.

Art was determined. We knew it could only be him tearing up the road towards us like the lead buffalo in a stampede. We also knew what he'd seen. "Pay-dirt, guys. One of the sons of bitches is in the trees." This time, even if it were last year's squirrel nest, we would be calling it an eagle. When we got to the spot Art clearly felt that a little hands-on direction would help. He clamped on to my shoulder like a winchman and aimed me towards a group of pines. And, sure enough, there it was. Not the most aesthetically pleasing view I've ever had, but the sigh of relief at seeing a real Bald Eagle must have sounded like air escaping from a balloon. I never thought I'd do it, but I hugged the big blancmange and promised to send him a picture of the bird; maybe even publish its photograph in a magazine alongside the tale of his good deed. Art filled up at

the sentiment but then blew it all when he said, "Gee fellas, I'm glad you foreigners are interested in our national emblem and not stupid dicky-birds."

August 2001
Dutch Birding

Mental
in Manitoba

My primary school was poor but it had one item that transcended make do and humdrum – it had a giant map of the world. It hung on Mr Mulvenna's wall behind his chair. Since he was the headmaster and his classes were conducted with an air of unyielding discipline, I could only gaze at it from afar. You only approached his desk when summoned. That would not be a good time to look away and say something like, "Please sir, how do you pronounce Nicaragua?" One day he was off sick and my class was left unsupervised, although given strict orders to behave by Mrs Donnelly from next door. That was my big chance. I offered to clean the blackboard for her – what a snivelling crawler – but only so I could commune with the map. I loved the deep blues of the Pacific east of the Philippines, and the tight rainbow of green, brown, and then white as you went from the Gobi Desert to the tops of the Himalayas. However, best of all was the vast green expanses of Russia and Canada. I looked up the key. 'Coniferous forest,' the legend said. Amazing. I thought of all the wild animals that must lurk in there. I remembered the term. I saved it up in my head and reserved it for special occasions when I wanted to impress. It was hard to impress Mr Mulvenna. He was fond of his red pen. He crossed out 'coniferous' in my homework. He underlined it, added a red exclamation mark, and then wrote in the margin, "Polar Bears are not coniferous – they are carnivorous."

Today, from a distance of 30,000 feet, I have finally seen what endless coniferous forest looks like. Below me lies the immense Canadian muskeg, its surface punctured by countless swamps, lakes and rapids stretching all the way from Labrador to Alaska. When I agreed to help lead this birdwatching tour to Manitoba I knew the scenery would be breathtaking, but I still wasn't prepared for the scale of it. You sit in a jet aircraft for hour after hour and the view remains the same. What changes are the time zones. Finally, unbroken agricultural prairie rolls into view and the captain announces that we are two hours from touchdown in Winnipeg. The airhostess stops her trolley in the aisle beside me and, with a cheesy smile, asks, "Brandy, sir?" I say, "It's too early in the morning; I've only just had breakfast." "But we are on Central Standard Time now," she replies, "It is actually two o'clock in the afternoon." "In that case I'll have a double," I say decisively, eager to show my appreciation of Air Canada's free booze.

It had been a long day. We got window seats for the slow train journey across the endless muskeg. Sometimes Hawk Owls are seen from the train. But not by our tour group. They fell asleep and I didn't have time to wake them up when I saw this. Well, maybe I didn't try too hard. Nuts to refunds.

A twin-track approach. On the one hand, best behaviour to create a false sense of responsibility; on the other, round-the-clock birding to tire them out. That way they will lie in bed until breakfast time and I'll be able to cram in several extra hours in the field, especially at Churchill where it's light by 0400hrs. Plus, there's a good dump nearby so I could get Thayer's Gulls in the early morning. Come to think of it, I could sleep in the van at the dump, as it might be light enough to see gulls after closing time at the British Legion bar in Churchill.

Such was plan A, explained in army cadet simplicity to co-leader Dave Allen as the two of us strode through Terminal 4 at Heathrow looking for the hapless birders who had booked to go on a Manitoba trip. God help them. Imagine being stuck with me for a fortnight. Sure, I know the birds reasonably well and even most of the best places, but think of the risks. Sleep deprivation guaranteed, one-eyed driving due to constant fence-post scanning for Upland Sandpipers and, after every good bird, a 'nip' to celebrate. Davis, whose concern for the welfare of clients is peerless, wasn't too supportive of my tactics. Right away he put the mockers on my intended use of tapes. On ethical and humanitarian grounds he said he couldn't agree that elderly tour participants with an average age approaching that of Methuselah should be subjected to The Prodigy and Oasis blasting at 20 watts per speaker during long van journeys.

On the first morning we hit the ground running. Tour leaders worry a lot about dipping out on difficult birds and we had toyed with the itinerary for months in an attempt to build in as many back-up sites as possible. We hoped to bag nail-biters such as Connecticut and Mourning Warblers quickly, which would take the pressure off and kick-start the trip with two prestige scalps right away. We needn't have worried. By 0900hrs we had a Mourning Warbler filling the telescope and singing its head off. Robert Bateman could not have conjured up a better composition for the views in fresh green aspen leaves. Smiles all round. Right then an awful realization dawned. I looked at the group as a heavy drizzle began to fall and the first of a zillion mosquitoes began to bite. They were happy as Larry, decked out in breathable, impermeable waterproofs, protected from bugs by Deet and dry-shod, thanks to Gore-Tex hiking boots. I surveyed the pair of us. We were already saturated, being bitten to buggery, and would have to wear wet trainers for days. The punters had outgunned us. Put us in the field and we do fine as ornithological sniffer dogs, but expect us to put brains before birding and we go to pieces.

A group is a curious thing. It starts out as a collection of strangers who come together only because they share a common interest and, within days, has transformed itself into an organism successfully adapted to a new environment. As far as I was concerned, it had evolved too fast. The more the punters saw, the more they wanted to see – and the earlier they got up in the morning. In a gross act of miscalculation I'd suggested that 'keenies' could meet at the van at 0500hrs for some pre-breakfast birding. The whole brood showed up before I did, binoculars sparkling in the dawn sunlight and not a hangover among them. That much I could take. At least outdoors I was in my element and could relax; indoors was becoming a problem. The blurb I'd been sent, entitled *Information for Leaders*, hadn't covered topics such as table etiquette, menu comprehension, and tipping. I was struggling with them all. One breakfast waitress, who wore an expression that would freeze the North Sea, was so formidable that we all ordered exactly the same thing for fear of someone being singled out and shot. On our last morning she mellowed from minus ten to minus nine. It was her way of warming us up to ensure a tip. When she opened our check and found my napkin sketch of the best way to tell Greater from Lesser Yellowlegs – a tip any birder would die for – she slammed the door behind us. For being smart, I scored a double whammy. The group thought I was mean.

At dinner in the next outpost I landed in more bother. Everybody ordered steak, which I thought about too, until I baulked at having to decide between 'rare', 'medium' or 'well done'. It was never like that at school dinners. In the end I played safe and chose trout but then the waiter asked how I wanted it cooked. The restaurant began to feel like the school examinations hall. I stalled, squirmed, the group turned to look, and I said "Well done." When the waiter arrived he whispered that he had taken the precaution of de-boning my dinner in case I thought it was meat and choked on the bones. From then on I stuck to omelettes.

That wasn't the worst bit. After the meal, Davis and I discovered that our luggage had been stolen. We returned to our motel room, which was like a new pin. No big green suitcase, no optics, no maps, tickets, passports or clean underwear. We were destitute. However, there was another side to the coin. Just as a group shares its joys, so too it shares its burdens. Calmly and thoughtfully, everybody rallied round. The manageress was summoned. Before the Mounties arrived, the group – some of whom seemed to be Grand Masters at *Cluedo* – suggested that the lady might like to open the adjoining rooms in case we had opened the wrong door. Impossible, the manageress said. It was late and guests in those rooms should not be disturbed.

We insisted. Reluctantly, she checked. No good news. She said the occupants were out but it was obvious from the state of the room that they were not the kind of people that you would want to know. Happily, a few moments later in front of four shocked witnesses, she was proved completely wrong. Or was she right?

August 1998
Birdwatch

What makes you
tick?

"You are going to COPELAND?" This was the reaction from (so-called) friends when Dave Allen and I broke the heretical news that we were going to spend a whole week of prime October time marooned on a small island in the Irish Sea a mere handful of miles from home. The expected glories of southwest Ireland were being abandoned in the hope that we might encounter good migration on our doorstep and maybe even find a rarity. Down the years Copeland Bird Observatory has added Fox Sparrow and Scarlet Tanager to the list of birds recorded in the Western Palaearctic but mostly its potential has never been realised – or so we hoped.

What did we have in mind? Theoretically, the third week of October on any small offshore island with a lighthouse and decent habitat ought to be a worthwhile bet for a range of scarce migrants. Yellow-browed Warbler, Red-breasted Flycatcher, Richard's Pipit and Lesser Whitethroat (remember, this is Northern Ireland) were all contenders. Of course, we'd both seen many of each before but to find just one on Copeland would be different. The lure of such undetected quality in our local area held a special fascination.

Theories are fine but in practice the weather was against us. A particularly poor October for passerine migration was apparently reducing observers elsewhere to boredom verging on dejection or, rumour had it, alcoholism. The scene on Copeland was entirely different. While it was clear that our ideas were going to have a hard time proving themselves in 1992, every migrant thrush was scrutinized, ears strained at each passing pipit and likely patches of cover were scanned with laser-guided precision. A loop tape in my brain repeated a simple message day and night: *find that bird*.

Confidence, optimism and perseverance are the qualities needed to do it and on the second day we struck gold. Like many of birding's religious moments, the final events leading to revelation happened as if by telepathy. It's true. Such as during a seawatch when you *knew* a Sabine's Gull was going to appear behind a line of Arctic Terns and – BINGO! – there it is. When that occurs I don't believe luck actually plays a significant part. An alert mind and the motivation to keep looking do most of the luck making. But it's no wonder the moment appears to be miraculous, almost dreamy. I guess it must be intuition of the third kind. In rarity hunting it feels like you can wish a bird into existence. Mind you, it is best not to be the sole observer when the Radde's Warbler you have been fantasizing about for years finally pops out of a bramble patch.

And so, at the end of a wet October morning, I stood overlooking a bushy gully for half an hour. Not a sausage. "Okay, if I was a Yellow-browed Warbler I'd pick a sheltered feeding spot in the lee of that willow bush, just about…there." It was as though I'd spirited the bird into existence. The wee gem was in that very spot. Holy Moses!

Of the dozens of Yellow-browed Warblers that Dave and I have seen, this was the sweetest, the nicest – the best. Why is it that you get so much more enjoyment from seeing a rare bird in your own place? That day I felt that Copeland was the centre of the Universe, that a real-life hero I'd admired from a distance had paid a visit to my home town and called to shake my hand. Such a lovely thought. Is that why beauty is always in the eye of the beholder? In looks, rare birds may not always outshine their commoner fellows but they sure have the power to make us the gift of a larger life.

From the island I could almost see the roof of my house on the mainland. Just beyond lay Belfast with its offices, industry and churning mass of mankind locked in busy lives. All this within sight of a tiny bird from Siberia that had created a memory to last a lifetime. Dave and I felt privileged, somehow connected to a higher existence. But, to be frank, we deserved it. We'd worked hard. We didn't know it at the time but we'd found the only Yellow-browed in Ireland in a week when nothing noteworthy was seen. Despite gloomy forecasts we hadn't submitted to a sense of doom or sank to lacklustre efforts in the field. The potential rewards of our chosen course were just too great.

To find one of these, all you have to do is think like a Yellow-browed Warbler. A bit of a no-brainer, then?

This autumn, don't let it be said that you didn't follow the same principle. Go out and make some memories.

The afterglow of the event was heart-warming, especially as there was no doubting that this was the occasion to open a certain bottle of celebratory rum that night. "Dave, I think I'll be happy now until the end of the winter." I said this in all sincerity, forgetting that a friend's insight may be more perceptive, which it was. "You've got to be joking McGeehan," he corrected. "You'll only be happy until tomorrow morning. I know what makes you tick."

September 1993
Birdwatch

Days
like this

A Little Bunting in Northern Ireland. How rare would that be? Oh, about as rare as a mountain range in Holland. That explained the late night heavy breathing phone call I got on Sunday 19 October 1997. A bird answering to the description of *Emberiza pusilla* – a mouse-like bunting creeping along the ground and going 'tick' every time it was nearly stepped on – was on Rathlin Island, five miles off the north coast of County Antrim. Not exactly convenient. Rathlin is a long lump of grey rock stuck out in the Atlantic embroidered with small green fields and smothered in rarity habitat. Yet nobody goes there. Why? Remember this is Ulster where there are fewer twitchers than there are moons around Saturn. Who found it? The honour went to young Liam McFaul, RSPB warden on the island. This was his first blockbuster and he was reputed to be incandescent with delight. However, he desperately wanted someone to travel over and confirm his suspicions.

That will do for the plot. Would I go for it, twitch it in other words? Well, it all depended. Mainly it depended on weighing up the chances of not seeing it. Was I prepared to devote a whole day to a long drive, a boat crossing, a stiff trek and hours of waiting and chewing nails only to taste the numbing disappointment of failure? Of course, the bird might be there and connecting with it could be as easy as, say, twitching a Rembrandt or a Van Gogh. You get directions to the museum, walk up a few flights of stairs and stand in line to get a guaranteed tickable view. The Old Master doesn't slink off and hide in an air conditioning duct, nor does it fly out of a window moments before you shuffle to the front of the queue. In betting terms, twitching an Old Master is a racing certainty. Which also means that, even though you are sure to clap eyes on the masterpiece and can commune with it for hours, the buzz of anticipation isn't anything like as memorable because the risk of not seeing it is nil. In the case of rarities, you are forced to gamble that the bird will remain long enough for you to bag it, which adds to the feeling of fulfilment when you do.

So, if tension matters, what makes a perfect day? Overcoming adversity for one thing. Think how Portugal must have felt when they came from behind to beat England 3–2 or France, equalizing against Italy in the 94th minute and then winning the final by a Golden Goal. A triumph made sweeter because it was uphill all the way. Plus, the storyline has to be good. There ought to be unexpected twists, glory should be wrung from impending failure and, at the very end, a wild coup de grâce to make the experience an indelible one for you and prompt those who weren't present to wet themselves.

It doesn't necessarily follow that an inauspicious beginning is the perquisite of a successful twitch. In fact, this time there was no ominous start – there was simply no start at all. For two days people hedged their bets and didn't go, convinced that the bird wouldn't be seen again. It was, of course. Each morning it was there, as regular as a clockwork mouse, scurrying up and down Liam's driveway until it received the fateful accolade of 'showing well and looking settled,' announced on the Irish birdline on Tuesday night. That did it. The bird was nowhere to be seen next day. And the day after that? Naturally that was when I planned to go. Okay, even I was a bit slow off the mark, but it's hard to be Speedy Gonzalez when your legal team is out of town and you have to represent yourself in a matrimonial hearing to plead for a day off housework.

Thursday morning saw Dundee Douglas and me crouching behind the pier wall in Ballycastle sheltering from the breakers that were pounding the strait between us and Rathlin. However, the weather was the least of our problems. Shepherded on to the boat with us was the Reverend Brendan Mulcahy, Ireland's only twitching minister. At the risk of sounding uncharitable, Blind Brendan was the last person we wanted to see. Don't get me wrong. He's a very nice man and mad keen on running for rarities. The difficulty is that rarities are even keener on running from him. He is the ultimate jinx. When, in conversation, he intimated that Little Bunting was his 'number one bogey bird' Dundee nearly leapt off the boat. But it was too late – by that stage we were adrift in the gale.

And then, like most rarities, it appeared - in the middle of nowhere.

Maybe it was the battle against heavy seas that made the island's boatmen look like a bunch of sulky old lions. Probably not – grumpiness is the normal Rathlin phenotype. The place has been invaded, sacked and occupied so many times that the locals don't know if they're descended from Scots, Irish, Asterix the Gaul or Palestinians. Given the Yasser Arafat dress sense of the guy we hired to transport us to Liam's house and the Arabic-like knotwork of fishing rope and clothes-line that held his car together, I think a Middle East ancestry is most likely. Actually, he turned out to be a Tasmanian who left Tasmania because it was bleak and damp, wandered the planet and wound up living on Rathlin because it reminded him so much of home. He was pretty friendly and left us right outside Liam's door. When he left and we spoke to Liam we wished the driver hadn't been so obliging. Liam said the Little Bunting invariably fed on the road, so our first task was to retrace the car's tracks and check if we'd run the bird over.

Well, it was neither dead nor alive on its favourite piece of terra firma, which was about the size of a penalty box. Furthermore, if gravel and grass verges were preferred habitat, then we were staring oblivion in the face. Have a look at the maths. Rathlin covers an area of 48 square miles. That's 64,480 square yards. Even if we divided up and gave Blind Brendan half to search, confident that with his record the bird was bound to be in our half, that still left 32,240 square yards to flog. And in only two hours before dark. Don't you just hate situations like this? Blitzkrieg is over and stalemate has begun. What should you do – embark on a cold search of endless habitat or stay put and endure the big sit? Logic dictates that if the bird liked one particular spot for three days then it will return; rarities are usually creatures of habit. You try hard to believe this. You concentrate on every movement. Over there – the flick of something small and brown in the undergrowth. This is the only action in an hour and it isn't even feathers. It's the swishing of a cat's tail in prime bunting habitat.

The big sit begat bedsores. Your mind drifts to other topics. Such as the plight of the Euro or that recent polls show fewer than one in four Britons remain in favour of continued membership of the EU. If I have a problem here on Rathlin then think of Tony Blair and the mountain of public opinion he has to climb. Actually, I made that bit up. I didn't want you imagining me as a zealot who thought only about birds. I think about religion too. After 90 desperate minutes I turn to prayer. I start to go gaga and promise God that I'll be a better person if I see the bird. I drew the line at that. Dropping hints to the Almighty wasn't going to make any difference, otherwise Blind Brendan would have found the bird ages ago.

And so the final curtain fell. Blind Brendan never did see a Little Bunting on Rathlin that day. His 100 percent record was maintained. He saw a Rustic Bunting instead. Fed up with sitting in one spot and doing an impression of Lot's wife, I went for a tramp further up the road and, just beyond where our taxi had turned, lurked the bird. It hopped up, called, flashed its telltale rusty flank streaks and sherry-coloured rump and a thundering extra time winner slammed home. Liam had misidentified the bird (unlike you?) but he'd been damn close; remarkably close when you consider he didn't have any field guide illustrations to base his guess on. That meant a great deal. Little Bunting would have been a major coup – but Rustic Bunting was a first for Northern Ireland. Aye carumba! Could a day that ended on a meteoric high possibly get better? That weekend it did. Rearrange these well-known terms to discover how: (i) dip, (ii) complete, (iii) mass. Excuse me for not putting the words into a proper sentence. It's just that some people over here are a bit touchy on the subject – you know what twitchers can be like.

June 2000
Dutch Birding

Autumn

Since I was little I've been hopeless at sums. Mathematics class scared me rigid. I recoiled from long division and escaped fractions by gazing through the classroom window at foliage on grand beech trees in the playground. The experience was transcendental although others, mainly teachers, considered it daydreaming. Master McDonald never gave me peace. He'd be writing something on the blackboard with his back to me, yet still catch me out: "McGeehan, quit gawking and get on with your work." Foxy Maguire, my mate, said the master yelled at me one morning when I wasn't even there. I was sick in bed with chicken pox.

A lifetime later my academic failure has receded. These days my wife says it is me that doesn't add up. She might be telling me that we are deeper in debt than Zimbabwe but I could be thinking about the weather. I am gone. It is autumn. A wind has sprung up in my face and I am transported to the west of Ireland.

A half-hour drive west of Killybegs, Donegal ends at the lonely parish of Malin Beg. Over the waves, the next settlement is Cape Spear, Newfoundland, Canada. Put another way, the land hereabouts marks the edge of Europe. Its terminus is a long heathery fist – Rocky Point – that punches out into the cold grey Atlantic.

Welcome to my Fair Isle. But not just mine. Over several autumns DIM Wallace and Dave Allen shared a tumbledown coastguard cottage with me. The Celtic Tiger whisked it away and into the hands of big money people from Dublin. 'Blowins,' the locals call them. In 2002, the news got worse. As well as being homeless, I risked being a lone musketeer. Not for long. Several untried substitutes wanted to try their hand at rarity hunting.

A new hostel opened and I tried it out on a pre-season warmup. The accommodation was great but reality hit hard next morning. I had to shave beside a naked German. When rumbled as a birdwatcher at a communal breakfast table, a teacher from Belfast pestered me about a mystery bird in her garden. Its features included 'a beak like a salmon' and a tail shaped like an ironing board (whatever that is). The hostel's death warrant was signed.

The house that was eventually secured ('Luxurious family residence with unrivalled sea views') was a nightmare. It was a nightmare because every word was true. It was a local family's summer palace. Expensive floor rugs and heirlooms were everywhere. Into this Hilton I was preparing to unleash a herd of blokes with muddy feet. Before Delta Force decamped I spent the night stowing delicate items into a garage. I also lifted the hall carpet.

By definition, rare birds are not easily found. The problem in the west of Ireland is that, most times, there aren't even common migrants through which to search for rarities. On previous trips, the sole flycatcher was a Red-breasted and the only warbler in a week was a Melodious. Out here, you need the faith of a Jesuit to find the few. Into the bargain, local weather is cruel and sheltering vegetation is sparse.

Should I stand under these sycamores a bit longer and risk falling into a hypnotic trance – or go seawatching where I am bound to see something? I decide to stay put. Resist the common for the chance of the uncommon. I play an imaginary round of Championship Birding. Wherever I look I see a rarity. Except there is nothing there. I keep hoping, trying to conjure up a bird through sheer willpower. This time I win the battle. A stem twitches and I track movement. The phantom is a Barred Warbler. Phew! The trip has a star. How had I found it? Luck, I suppose. Up to now I was alone. Free to not worry if I didn't unearth something better. What I miss will remain a mystery.

The troops arrived and were buoyed up by my tally. Not just the Barred Warbler but a list of Irish notables too: Lesser Whitethroat, Pied Flycatcher, Common Rosefinch. Now everyone wanted to be part of the action. Tuesday 24 September began quietly, very quietly. By mid-afternoon the day was dragging. Nothing had been found and local sheepdogs were snoozing in the sun. Birding degenerated into a siesta, prompting some of the gang to slouch off and photograph the Barred Warbler. The rest of us drifted away. An hour later we wished that we'd drifted into the grill of a speeding lumber truck, which would have prevented us

from hearing the news that we'd spent 60 minutes up the road from a Citrine Wagtail. The apparition had beamed down from a clear blue sky and stayed long enough to be digitised. Then it became a phoenix. The rest of us had dipped.

The images were spellbinding but also the stuff of nightmares. Through a black night I thought less about the slim chance of the bird being relocated and more about the three Rs: the razor, the rope, the revolver. Autumn had done the thing that I most dread. It had spat me in the face and dashed my hopes of finding a sizzling rarity. To non-birders, these emotions are hard to grasp. A psychiatrist would probably graph my feelings inside a Venn diagram – a set of circles listing motivation, expectations, frustration, palpitations and constipation. Is birding out to get me? I am ready to face the facts. I am a loser. My reward for walking for days – years – around this dump has been little enough. Now the best bird ever had eluded me. Autumn is a counter-intuitive season. It promises so much but the consequences of not enjoying the hunt are deep crushing pessimism. Depression even.

I tried hard to feel that defeat was not inevitable. I summoned up some of the phrases that have got me through sticky patches before. When times are hard, you need to hum a dreary song with some hope in it – not a haunting melody about suicide. Furthermore, rarities are tabloid birds. They make headlines once and then fade like yesterday's news. So I need to live in the world, not in my head.

Next morning I shrugged off group therapy and went outdoors. If anyone knew the best spots to search it was I. The barren

Citrine Wagtail: it's not what it looks like, it's how it makes you feel.

landscape could be an asset. A vagrant wagtail might not have too many places to hide. Before the cornflakes got as far as my small intestine I heard the call. A glorious piercing sound, reminiscent of a Skylark on helium. I felt that I had survived a near miss. Not with a mercurial rarity but with birding's dark competitive side. Autumn is a pressure cooker that, when it recedes into winter, leaves you relieved to look at gulls.

December 2002

Dutch Birding

A serious
problem

It is really surprising how many rudderless people there are in the world, especially among the crowd gathered at Rocky Point, Donegal, one day last September. The boys were there in strength of course, with cohorts from the upstanding north and outlying southern provinces.

The stuff was pouring past and it was hard enough to pick out the odd Sabine's Gull or Leach's Storm Petrel from the passing horde without being hampered by the babble emanating from the likes of Seamus McStammer, Freddie Fourbellies and young Felim (known as Kling Felim to one and all). All I can conscientiously say about the latter as a sea-watcher is that you can have him.

Here's why. Just as I am getting screamer looks at a close adult Pomarine Skua (perfect tail, yellow nape, full breast band – the works) he almost spontaneously combusts beside me. "POSSIBLE LONG-TAILED SKUA IN THE SKY!" "Where?" Near that Gannet." "I don't see a Gannet - anything else?" "Em, got the puffy white cloud?" "Nope." "Well, the Gannet's directly below it." "Forget the feckin' Gannet, where's the skua? Hold on a minute, is it anywhere near that plane?" "Yes, that's what I mean - the plane is a Fairy Gannet." "Look, I'm not into aircraft ID. Where the hell is

the skua?" "It's over the sea now, shearing." "Going left or right?" "It's banking." "Felim, for Christ's sake, say which direction it's flying. Banking is what you do with your money and shearing is what your old man does to his sheep. Wait, I've got it. It's just an Arctic Skua – so you were only half wrong." "Thanks, I thought that's what it was anyway. What took you so long?"

As the day wore on, birds were seen "flying over the horizon" (even the Hubble telescope cannot see that far) and "from left to right." That one really cracks me up. It's like describing something travelling head first and tail last. Why use three words when one will do? What's wrong with flying *right*?

While waiting for other putative goodies to gather themselves after "slipping over a wave", there was the further time-wasting distraction of guessing the words in McStammer's gappy utterances. "Fa, fa, fa …" became not falcon, fallopian tubenose or even fast-moving something-or-other but (in the end) "phalarope". Luckily for him it hung around long enough to lay an egg so we all got on it.

The problem is no less acute with stationary objects. Such as: "Blimey! There's an Osprey perched in that pine." "Where?" "Are you blind? At the end of the bare branch." "Ah, got it now – you mean perched in the Norway Spruce."

Yes, for a generation that is so interested in splitting bird species, it is amazing how much lumping of other flora and fauna goes on. A woodland edge comprising hazel, ash, holly, oak and birch becomes "those trees over there", while a complex herb layer of bluebells, anemones, primroses and orchids is simply referred to as "the deck". Aesthetics of the non-avian world apart, it can actually be useful to know the names of a few vegetation types as this will help in giving directions to good birds that may lurk therein.

Another autumn a ragged company was tramping across the windswept heathery summit of Cape Clear Island in pursuit of a Richard's Pipit when Botany Bill spots it disappear into a yellowish tuft of grass. "It's over here," he shouts, "in that tiny patch of reeds."

I suppose you are wondering where all this is leading. Well, it's simple. The next time you see something interesting and are under pressure to give a good bead to it before someone gets overheated and decides to brain you out of frustration, remember the following. Don't mumble or dither. Think brevity and think precision. Spit out where it is and what it is doing. Look for reference points – but if there aren't any, say so. "There's nothing near it. I'll shout when it passes something," is better than, "Look where I'm looking." And for heaven's sake keep watching. Don't take your eye off it until at least one other person has located it. Only then put your bins down so you can point it out to the other dimwits who haven't seen it yet. That way, you'll have support in case of trouble.

Believe it or not, personal survival may depend upon your direction-giving abilities, as Vic the Slick knows from bitter experience. Vic, then a handsome guy and a great handyman with women despite being knee-high to a corgi, was the last-but-one off the trawler that night. The boys had been on a pelagic trip and now I was doing the customary flashlight check for items of forgotten kit. Vic was shifting his gear into Freddy Fourbellies' car prior to joining the rest of the gang in the pub. From dark recesses three decks down I didn't pay much attention when I heard his first muffled call ("Freddy, I'm splitting,") that I took to mean he wasn't bothering with the pub and was off to the B&B.

I got more curious when this was followed by: "Freddy, I'm down to my last inch." Perhaps he was skinny-dipping in the harbour? Actually, it sounded as if he was up to some titillating tomfoolery that I preferred to know nothing about. Finally there was a yell: "PULLUS!" Good man Vic – I assumed he had found the juvenile Rock Pipit that had been dazzled earlier by the ship's lights and had fluttered below decks. Maybe he had it cornered and needed a hand to catch it? I rushed up the ladders but was unprepared for the sight that met my eyes.

There was Vic the Slick, one foot on the harbour wall, the other on the trawler, his manhood about to split asunder. Fourbellies grabbed his arm, I got a leg, and between us we saved him for womankind and birding. If he'd used just a little common sense and shouted better information, we could have spared him the wrenching experience. As Fourbellies succinctly put it, "Jesus, Vic, what's wrong with the word HELP?"

July 1996
Birdwatch

Practice on this. Without pointing, explain to a member of the public the precise location of the bird in the photograph.

The buck
starts here

There are plenty of words for it: mistake, error, misidentification. Superficially, they describe the simple act of looking at a bird and calling it the wrong species. But what if the act is a public one, done in front of witnesses – or worse, corrected later by hordes of birders who have travelled miles to watch, not a Pechora Pipit but just a misidentified Meadow Pipit?

Then words like 'mistake' form just the tip of a murky ice-berg that has the sub-text of 'failure,' 'object of scorn' and 'stringer' written all over it. Human nature is a vulnerable thing so it can be hard to take such criticism, especially when it is proffered with the benefit of hindsight.

Of course, everybody makes mistakes – you, me, Lars Jonsson. They are an unavoidable part of our learning curves, so it's unfortunate when they carry a stigma that reflects upon an individual's competence and integrity. No point in taking things personally? Well, people do, although they shouldn't, and yet sometimes we may be partly responsible for the consequences of our own actions.

1984 was my year of incompetence. That August, I was one of many who saw themselves as the hapless victims of mass

hallucination when a Least Sandpiper masqueraded for a whole week as a Temminck's Stint at Ballycotton. "Won't make that mistake again, will never trust someone else's identification again, will always look properly in future – I damn well mean it this time." These were the sorts of hand-wringing sentiments I used to salve my conscience.

Then in October I found a wing-barred *Phylloscopus* warbler on Cape Clear Island and promptly misidentified it. I thought I had stumbled into an Arctic Warbler but it was a Greenish.

With the lessons of the Least Sandpiper debacle still supposedly fresh, I had screwed up again – and in public. It should have been a proud moment for me, but instead I felt robbed, bushed, beaten. It wasn't the mistake *per se* that hurt; it was a feeling of doom and personal demise. There is no point in being sensitive about this anymore – for one thing, you lot now know – but no amount of mitigating circumstances softened the blow at the time. Looking back, there were several nails in my coffin right from the outset.

I'd let a preconceived notion of what I imagined an Arctic Warbler must look like colour my view. Armed with a few quick

Sometimes ordinary, familiar species – such as this Meadow Pipit – seen in unusual circumstances can present more of an identification challenge than many birders think.

glimpses of a long supercilium, pale legs (but actually mid-brown) and a 'heavy' bill, everything either seemed to fit – or was made to fit, subconsciously of course. From that point my mind was closed. Even when the bird obliged and gave much

better views it was too late: the blinkers were on. Finally, when I did develop nagging misgivings, the unquestioning acceptance of other birders' supporting opinions was enough to stifle any further need to look afresh at the empirical evidence fly-catching in front of me. Then it called and yelled its identity into our thick skulls.

Although it pains me to admit it, I didn't keep an open mind for long enough, didn't want to re-evaluate the bird's features once I'd committed myself to an identification and wasn't honest about the limitations of my experience and hence of my opinion. If I'd remembered the maxim: 'Imagination is no substitute for experience', I might have watched the bird more critically and encouraged others to do the same. So, in the end, I reckoned that I deserved to take the blame for being the architect of a shambles.

Since then, I've made many more mistakes. A few in public but most in private. I've failed to tell Goshawk from Sparrowhawk, Little Auk from Puffin and called Pomarine Skua everything from Long-tailed Skua to Basking Shark fin. However, there are big differences. Nowadays, I look upon mistakes as opportunities to correct impressions, home in on differences and actually build confidence and expertise. For example, how *do* you tell a Pomarine Skua at long range? Test out a few criteria of your own, get it wrong lots of times and eventually you'll start hitting the target. Oddly enough, you might find that gut reaction gained through familiarity with the species *that the bird is not*, may be the best guide.

Gradually, I've learned that making mistakes is nothing to be ashamed of. It's not a weakness or failing – so long as it leads to self-questioning and a renewed understanding of where you went wrong. However, for this process to succeed, you have to be scrupulously honest with both yourself and other birders.

What do I mean by honest? Honest means seeing what is actually there rather than what you expect to see. It means being frank about your doubts. Look for yourself. Play devil's advocate. Get uncertainty off your chest: so what if you are ultimately wrong? Better not to brood about it and sleep soundly.

One birder whose honesty impressed me was Martin Blick. He noticed, but didn't identify, Britain's first Double-crested Cormorant. His account of the bird's discovery in *Birding World* began: "I won't forget 11 January 1989 in a hurry. It was the day that I looked at a first for the Western Palaearctic and got it wrong." That statement took courage to write and had another ingredient that shouldn't be underestimated in such situations – a sense of humour.

When you refine your thoughts and commit pen to paper, even greater honesty is required. Be truthful. Don't mix real life observations with book representations. And don't be afraid to leave gaps. Gaps, if airbrushed over with conjecture or bridged with speculation, have a habit of turning into crevasses into which the wannabe identifier disappears without trace. So go easy and make sure each step is based on solid ground.

Oh, one last thing – the bird in the photograph. It's really a Buff-bellied Pipit, the sort of major find that could lurk anywhere in Britain or Ireland during winter. Did you fall for the Meadow Pipit misidentification? Then, well done, you've just made a mistake!

December 1994
Birdwatch

Island life

Cape Clear Island is about the optimum size for a relaxing holiday. It is roughly three miles long with a rugged coastline and picturesque switchbacks of steep, narrow roads that snake up, down and around all corners of the island. It also has three pubs. Except for the last attribute, it is really too big and hilly for a bird observatory, with its only area of flat green space reserved for snooker. However, it's the best we've got, and although many autumn trips score poorly for rarities there is no shortage of adrenaline rushes.

The most frequent of these is caused by telepathy, which, because radio signals are often disrupted by the island's topography, serves as the best form of inter-birder communication. This works as follows. After two hours at a recognized hotspot in the north end, you still haven't met a sinner. You walk past the only shop, where the phone rings incessantly for five minutes. The shop is closed and no one is at home to take the call. A note scribbled on a piece of card is lying flat on the counter but you can't read it through the window. It is probably proclaiming news of a Tennessee Warbler at the south end where everyone else is – and they are watching it right now. You feel this in your bones so, naturally, you take to your heels. In fact it was Mary O'Driscoll ringing to order some groceries and the note was from Paddy Timothy to his wife Kathleen saying: "Gone to Skibbereen for tractor parts. Clean the cowshed."

When radios crackle intermittently into life they may bring tidings, not of good birds, but of a widespread outbreak of 'umbrella syndrome'. This is unrelated to the weather and most often occurs on birdless days about an hour before the arrival of the daily mail boat at three o'clock. These are the hallmarks. Me, upon hearing an incoherent splutter on the airwaves, "Come in Marconi, what's your news and position? Over." "The news is that there is no news. My current position is in Fatso's with a pint of Murphy's in my right hand. Over." "You mean you've folded – you big umbrella. Over." "Quite right. It's dead around here. Unlike you, I'm not Don Quixote, wasting good drinking time by wandering around tilting at Winchats. Fatso says can he pull you a glass of his best? Over." Naturally, I decline the offer, saying, "Where are the boys? Don't tell me they're checking the bushes beside the harbour? Over." "How did you guess? Cheers. Over and out."

To the uninitiated visiting birdwatcher the miraculous afternoon discoveries of major rarities in the harbour bushes seem inexplicable. Ever since a Rose-breasted Grosbeak was found here at two o'clock on 7 October 1962, the area has retained its mysterious attraction. Except it's hardly a mystery that, while hanging around waiting for any incoming female Swedish reverse migrants or nubile New World overshoots, up to 20 blokes with binoculars may happen to chance upon the odd

This brought me out in rose-breasted goosebumps.

rarity in the only available cover nearby. During lean spells of migration the assembled male birding corps is anything but averse to extra-curricular activities: offering assistance with bags, giving directions, bike-pushing and providing an escort service to hostels, campsites and, perchance of an evening, the bar (where knowledge of optics comes in handy, especially measures of vermouth and brandy).

After dark, one of the most public-spirited and tourist-friendly members of the well-lubricated birding team is always Victor Victorious. Of course his real name is not Victorious but something Italian like *vermicelli*, and I hear he comes from Sicily, although he also lived in Brooklyn for some years. He is a handsome guy of maybe 20-odd, has hair blacker than a yard up a chimney and a humorous way of looking at people. Well, imagine the chemistry when, at the end of a lovelorn European tour, an American Empress from New York set foot on Cape Clear. Victor was in with the blarney quicker than you could order a pint. In fact, he was given a bit of a home run with the Empress, to whom everyone else gave a wide berth. She had gorgeous hair and gleaming white gnashers, but enough chins to make a fire escape and she disposed of pizzas the size of manhole covers. Nevertheless, beauty is in the eye of the beholder, and while Victor Victorious hadn't underestimated her physical

Rush hour, Cape Clear Island, County Cork.

attributes, rumour had it that his interest centred more upon her scent of collateral. There was no doubting that she was an impressive piece of real estate, so much so that, to everyone else, she became known as the Empress State Building. She also proved to be one of Uncle Sam's foremost bottle-women with a thirst greater than Red Rum. All of which explains why, for the duration of her stay, Victor was scarcer in the field than a flock of Slender-billed Curlews.

The day that the Empress finally set sail, Victor was spotted by certain parties by the names of Blind Billy and Sniper Sid. He was slumped against a wall and so shattered with alcohol and sleep deprivation that he was gripping his binoculars purely to arrest the shake in his hands. This made him a perfect candidate for the Cape Clear Island hill climb. I am reliably informed that, upon observing the condition of Victor, Blind Billy and Sniper Sid manoeuvred themselves until they knew he could see them, at which instant they took off up the nearest hillside like two men who'd just seen a first for the Western Palaearctic. Naturally, this resulted in near fatal palpitations for Victor who struggled, like a soul on the verge of death, to the top of the hill.

Here he was met by a scene – not of pandemonium – but suspicious contentment. He'd been hoodwinked and he knew it. The odd thing was, he felt better for it and even Blind Billy's attempt at continuing the joke, "Say Victor, is that a whale offshore or has the Empress just gone for a swim?" made him pleased that the boys could see he'd only gone AWOL for the last three days, and hadn't been mortally wounded in action.

November 1996
Birdwatch

Semi-identified
Sandpiper

Saturday dawned wet and miserable and accompanied by the sound of cartoons wafting upstairs. The kids were up already. It takes a crowbar to rouse them on weekdays, yet Saturday morning fever grips them like a call-to-arms. Ten, nine, eight, seven – the final seconds of peace tick away, then it hits: "DAD." "Please, I'm very tired, give me a break – wake your mother."

"But dad, *British Birds* has just arrived." Instantly I spring out of bed, vault the stairs in one go and turn straight to the 'monthly marathon' quiz photograph. Damn, it's a tricky sandpiper. I order the wife out of bed to make breakfast, fail (deliberately) to hear the baby crying and turn up the radio to drown out requests for paternal assistance.

Breathless, I make it to the attic unscathed and begin to study the photograph. Initial thoughts suggest it's a juvenile, so I should have plenty of reference material. I ransack bookshelves and rummage through boxes of slides labelled: 'Peeps – various.' By nine o'clock I've decided I know what it is: a White-rumped Sandpiper. Easy peasy – a gleam of white rump plumage is discernible. I shave, slurp some coffee, begin to feel properly awake and sneak a confirmatory look. Panic. The smidgen of white feathering is on the lower back – not the rump. So my

first guess is dead and buried. Idiot! Loud calls from downstairs precipitate a coercive encounter with wife and kids.

"What in the name of God are you doing up there?" "It's a kind of ornithological crossword." "Can't you leave it to later?" "Definitely not. I have to work it out before any of the boys do. I don't want any of that lot beating me to it." "So, you aren't coming shopping then?" "Nope, can't make it."

For this refusal I am given two hours of housework that I complete in five minutes (dishes put away wet, duvet flounced over bed but neither sheets nor pillow-cases changed). More coffee is made and carried to the attic. Real work resumes. So, a clean-breasted peep with essentially monochrome upperparts. The cold and colourless back tones eliminate both Least Sandpiper and Long-toed Stint. Based on the straight short bill and not even a hint of rufous on the scapulars, it's clearly not a Western. It doesn't have a split supercilium, mantle stripes or solid dark centres to the lower scapulars so I can also forget about Little Stint.

All of which brings the choice down to a two horse race between the troublesome twosome of Asian Red-necked Stint versus North American Semipalmated Sandpiper. I can't see

Solve the identification of the bird in this mystery photograph to impress your mates and enhance your reputation. So don't get it wrong.

the feet to check for semipalmations between the toes and sense impending despair. I rock back in the chair, inhale deeply from a fag and attempt to extricate some earwax but instead dislodge hot cigarette ash that almost ignites my ponytail.

Out of confusion comes concentration. I try a quicker route to identification. It's called cheating. I phone an expert on seaweeds. "Hi Bob, I've got a photo here of green wrack and I think it might be an American species of seaweed. Can it be identified – is there such a thing as Chesapeake Bay Bladder-wrack or Connecticut Kelp?"

"What's in the background? No, I'm afraid I can't make out the Statue of Liberty or the Golden Gate Bridge." Ah well, it was worth a try.

Hunger strikes. I think about organically grown potatoes and a vegetarian casserole but instead opt for expediency. I take two frozen slices of white bread, slap a piece of ham in between and add a dollop of tomato ketchup. Lunch emerges from the microwave resembling the Japanese flag. I eat it while deciphering the following Per Alström identification text: 'On Red-necked, the sides of the crown are almost invariably distinctly greyer and more finely streaked than the centre of the crown; a dark central ridge is thus formed. On Semipalmated, the crown is very evenly coloured and streaked, creating a distinct capped appearance.'

Half an hour of scrutinizing the bird's head leaves me scratching mine. I'm undecided as to which plumage interpretation fits best. Stalemate is reached when I discover that concolorous ear-coverts and nape are strongly indicative of Red-necked. I can't make up my mind about this feature either. Cross-referencing of upperparts patterns and primary projections ends in another cul-de-sac and by late afternoon I am reduced to swishing my ponytail and fiddling with my earring for amusement while praying for divine intercession. Maybe that's what guided me to conclude that the subterminal dark crescent (like a Cupid's arrow – mmm, I wonder how the shopping trip's going?) behind the pale fringe of the innermost greater covert could be used to separate all Semipalmateds from Red-neckeds in the many

photos I had now examined. And Lars Jonsson's plate agreed – phew!

Saturday night. A phone call from a studious colleague. His opening question is music to my ears.
"Have you seen the latest *British Birds*?
"No, it hasn't arrived yet. What about it?"
"That's a pity. I was going to ask what you made of the quiz photograph – it's really tough this month. I spent all morning on it and I'm completely stuck."
"Gosh, I wish I could help. Bring it along tomorrow and I'll have a look at it."

I call for him early, just after dawn. He produces the magazine within minutes of getting into the car. Outside it's damp and foggy. In the half-light you can scarcely see to drive. He holds the page open and I risk a quick look. "Peep," I say immediately, before switching my gaze back to the road. "Yes, I thought so too," he volunteers, "but which one?"

I ask him to describe the pattern of the greater coverts. Is the innermost visible? It is. Good. Can he hold it up again? I twist my head, peer intently for three seconds and then pause briefly (to suggest ornithological omniscience is being tapped). "Straightforward Semipalmated," I declare emphatically. He is gob-smacked. It is only now I realise that, until next month when the answer is published, I can look forward to even less sleep than before.

October 1994
Birdwatch

Warden's report

"Anthony has a last chance to improve" **by Mrs McGeehan**

Capricorns are solid, hard-working types, loyal and true, and can be relied upon by others to see them through: in sickness or in health, richer or poorer, until death (or birdwatching) do part. Most Capricorns also have the misfortune to be born in January, which right away poses an annual challenge for an airy-fairy Piscean husband. Would he, as usual, forget my birthday? He did. Less than a month into the New Year and already his remorse sounded like a broken record. I said, "You can stick your excuses where the sun don't shine. If a rare bird had turned up on the same date you would have remembered that all right."

Then I set him a test. I said, "On what date did you find Northern Ireland's first American Herring Gull?" "The afternoon of 22 March 1990." I knew he was right (I'll tell you why in a minute). "And what else happened that day?" A dreamy look came over him that fitted the blank space between his ears. "Can't remember – should I?" I moved in for the kill. I said, "If eight pounds and ten ounces had come out from between your legs in Belfast City Hospital at nine o'clock in the morning I think the birth of your son would be etched more clearly in your mind and probably in a few other places as well." According to independent sources, that exit line put paid to an impending winter birding weekend for which he was about to ask permission.

Rarely observed events in the birding calendar. No 1: children's birthdays in autumn.

Years later it became obvious who was stealing potatoes from whom.

The kids are now of an age where they are starting to ask awkward questions such as "Why did God make birds?" – something I too have thought about – but so far, they seem intrigued by their father's activities. To his credit, anything in the natural world sets him off. So, while my children may arrive at school wearing odd socks and without lunchboxes, they can draw and write about bats, frogs and seals, based upon first-hand experience. However, the mysteries of the bird world – migration and the like – are taking longer to sink in.

Him, pointing out stars on a clear night to his daughter, aged eight. "That's Polaris - the pole star – and there's Orion. Birds can navigate by the stars and follow them all the way to Africa so they don't get lost." A large fact for a young brain, but she seemed impressed and even asked the question: "Why is it called Orion?" Her younger brother, in a voice that expressed surprise at her stupidity, interjected: "Why do you think – after Ryan Giggs, of course." "Thanks," his sister said, enlightened. Kids one, father nil.

In the rest of the animal kingdom spring is a time for simple creatures to give themselves a good shake and stir out of winter hibernation. Not so in our house. Lethargy arrives with lengthening daylight and is most acute on Sunday afternoons. As 'dawn starts' get earlier, he gets groggier when he arrives home at lunchtime.

And then what? "I just need an hour's peace to do my bird notes." I told him he should come back an hour earlier if he wanted to do that. I said, "Normal husbands regard Sundays as quality time to spend with their wife and family. You slump in the nearest chair and have a conversational ability that ranks lower than an 'I Speak Your Weight' machine. Enough is enough. I never intended to be married to a zombie." He panicked when I referred to him in *the past tense*. The message got through. He bought a Dictaphone.

As the dreaded autumn drew nearer, his performance slipped badly in several departments. Missing his daughter's birthday because of a Rock Thrush was the last straw. This was a watershed in our relationship. A woman's principles and inner desires are often hard to reconcile but now, in the prime of life, I realised why I needed Anthony. Quite simply, this is the man who makes me faint. Unlike his friends, he has remained slim and hirsute. Well worth fighting for. I decided on a 'New Approach' and embarked on a campaign to transform him – to make him see that there is more to life than birding.

First, I gave him free reign with the calendar. A week on Cape Clear Island in October and every Sunday free until December. However, Saturday mornings in bed were compulsory. He agreed. I sent him to get a haircut, gave him money for a new pair of jeans (still 30 inch waist, think about that) and went through his 'wardrobe' like a dose of salts. His dress sense seemed to be modelled on the People's Republic of China for, apart from things I'd bought him, everything was either black or navy blue. Tracksuit bottoms, cardigans, khaki-coloured long johns and rancid dandruffy woolly hats – I chucked the tat in a pile between the wash basket and bin. The sight of this gave him apoplexy. He started to shake like a palm frond in a hurricane and stammered: "Don't do anything with that lot. They always look clean. The dark colours don't show the dirt. If you wash them they might shrink and I'll need the long johns for seawatching later this winter."

They say anger is the most difficult emotion to manage but I think, in the circumstances, I acquitted myself rather well. I had a little speech prepared for such an eventuality and now, taking my elbows out of the dishwater in the kitchen sink, I let him have it. I said, "You know that little proverb you are fond of reciting, the one that goes 'It is a sad house where the hen crows louder than the cock'? Well, it's true. It also means you have two choices: move out or buck up. As for your statement in connection with this pile of rags – what 'seawatching later this winter'? January is a long way off but it is important to me for another reason. A wrong answer now could spell divorce."

He's working on it.

January 1996
Birdwatch

Research
bureau

He looked every bit the proud owner of the best telescope around. As he screwed his left eye shut like some diurnal Patrick Moore and squeezed his right against a small fortune in optical technology, the image that seared his retina confirmed it. Which just goes to show how wrong you can be.

It seems so natural now, but it only dawned on me recently that until I forced myself to *keep both eyes open* my gaze wasn't relaxed and I wasn't getting the most from my telescope. More to the point, eyestrain headaches had more to do with how I used a telescope rather than the length of time I spent looking through one. Check if the following symptoms sound familiar. After protracted one-eyed staring you switch from telescope to binoculars. Your vision is wonky – not double vision exactly, just a blurred synchronization of a proper image. You persist with binoculars and normal vision gradually returns – until you clamp your eye back on the telescope. After an intensive seawatching weekend the problem becomes so acute that you need seasickness pills to drive home. Why should this be? Not surprisingly, the answer is that one of your eyes is temporarily not focusing. What is surprising is that the one affected is the one you have been closing!

"How do you manage to use a camera yet keep both eyes open?" It was an innocent question. The person I was speaking to – a busy professional photographer – told me that he didn't use to. He said that he had to learn the skill for the sake of his eyesight. In the past he had suffered such blinding headaches that he couldn't work. Put simply, he'd contorted his eyeball through constant pressure. Cripes! Let's be selfish about this. Is there anyone on this planet who values their eyesight more than a birder? Of course not. Hence it was fear that drove me to master the technique of always keeping my 'non-telescope eye' open.

The aim is to trick your brain into ignoring what you register through one eye, so that it doesn't interfere with the image you see down the telescope with the other. 'Down' is an important word here, for an angled telescope makes the learning process easier – your free eye will be looking downwards at uninteresting foreground, rather than forwards at the same scene your telescope eye sees.

I find that broad-bodied telescopes – especially when padded out by a neutral-coloured case – assist, since they block out even more of the immediate foreground.

The first published photograph of the virulent strain of Bird Flew – or TGS, Telescope Glare Syndrome. The downside of kitting yourself out like a twitcher-come-terrorist is that birds spot your telescope's reflection at a mile range.

With practice, you'll succeed. And believe me, it's worth persevering. Here's a short cut that might help. I use a homemade cap (plastic tablet bottle lined with towel grip for a snug fit) to protect the telescope's viewing eyepiece. This gadget is attached to the body of the telescope with pliable rubber-coated electrical wire. It is easy to bend the wire and position the cap at the side of the telescope, thus blotting out your free eye's view of the ground at your feet. A word of caution. Obliterating the foreground completely could prevent you from finding a foot-crawling Lanceolated Warbler with one eye while the other is busy identifying a Fea's Petrel at two miles range.

Last autumn I witnessed an eminent ornithologist sitting on cold wet rocks while seawatching. Does a mother's advice count for nothing? How many times in childhood were we told never to do this? The youth of today have the answer – booster seats. Made of moulded polystyrene and adorned in fabric depicting scenes from nursery rhymes, they are all the rage with the new generation who use them to get a better view from the back seat of the family car. They also make wonderful seawatching seats. Lightweight, seemingly indestructible and, mirabile dictu, the longer you sit on them the warmer your buns get. Here's the rub. I can't see too many of you Gary Cooper types staying long enough in Mothercare to buy one. I had thought of marketing a camo version for the Ray Mears market but instead I've devoted my energies to cracking a more serious problem – the bird-scaring effect of TGS (Telescope Glare Syndrome).

Are you aware of this? I don't believe many people are, although you have almost certainly experienced it. How many times have you scanned a group of birds, locked on to something interesting only to see *that very bird* become unsettled and fly off? Or, as you pan along a line of roosting gulls, your progress sets off an awakening wave of Mexican proportions? What is happening in these situations is that birds catch sight of light reflecting off the telescope's objective lens that shines straight at them like a mirror. No wonder they scarper.

Is there a remedy? Well, yes there is. However, before I give you the bad news – it costs money – I want to set the record straight. First I tried to interest the BTO in affixing Polaroid contact lenses to all birds handled for ringing. They refused. Next I smeared Vaseline *on my own objective lens* to see if that dispersed the light. I couldn't see a thing. Finally I managed to interest an optical manufacturer in developing a self-attaching neutral density filter that does the job perfectly. Place your order using the form inside the back cover. All cheques payable to BFH Ltd. Due to continuing research, no proceeds go to conservation. God bless you.

April 1996
Birdwatch

Name
Game

Field identification of Long-tailed, Arctic and Pomarine Skuas has long been considered difficult. In particular, distinguishing between juveniles of each is complicated by their enormous variability, from almost wholly dark to very pale-headed. This article discusses those features that can help separate the least common species – Long-tailed – from Arctic Skua, its most similar congener. Juvenile Long-tailed Skuas are generally greyer in tone than juvenile Arctics, with somewhat longer central tail feathers. The palest individuals –

EDITOR: Hold on a minute, this stuff has a familiar ring to it – haven't I seen it somewhere before?

AMG: Not really. It is my unique and personal summary of known identification criteria, which updates and sheds new light on the subject. A sort of state-of-the-art précis.

EDITOR: Pardon? If I'm not mistaken, this has been copied from other identification papers and Lars Jonsson's text in *Birds of Europe*. All you have done is mix it up a bit.

AMG: What's wrong with that? A lot of bird identification writing is done like that. Once this article is published it will look like I came up with the novel discoveries. Furthermore, I can then go into print and even reference myself. The more I repeat the attributions to my name, the harder it will be to work out who did the real work.

EDITOR: WHAT'S WRONG? Heavens above man, don't you think you should at least credit your sources or put *their* texts in quotation marks? You are stealing other people's observations. In my book that amounts to plagiarism. Have you no buttock-clenching sense of embarrassment?

AMG (sweat popping from every pore): But no-one will ever notice –

EDITOR: When I started reading this I expected to see some fresh material. I thought that, after all those years shivering on Irish headlands, you must have learned something. But no. All I get is smoke and mirrors employed to sidestep a taboo: 'Credit where credit is due.' And another thing. You claim to have seen 23 juvenile Long-tailed Skuas in one day. That's more than I have seen in my life. If they really were Long-taileds, surely you can explain how they were identified? Have you an original thought in your head? If so, get on with it before I let this page for advertising (to an optical company – I'm beginning to think that you could use their services).

AMG (chastened): Gulp. Thanks for the lifeline and advice. In fact, most of the birds you refer to were seen well enough to confirm identification based on well-publicized plumage details. I saw them really well – honest.

EDITOR: In other words, published information bagged them for you.

AMG: Yes, but after a while I started to notice that they had a different way of flying, behaving, and conducting themselves. In the end, I reckoned that, based on a combination of shape, manner of flight and foraging actions, it was entirely possible to be confident of identification before closer views confirmed it. The bottom line is that I might have stumbled into something. So, if you think you can stand the wind and cold, here are a few ideas to try out on an autumn seawatch.

EDITOR: Something concrete at last. I hope the pictures are good.

AMG: Em, photographs don't help, although video would show what I am talking about. It's a Real World thing. When you see a juvenile skua start to dip-feed it is Game Over.

EDITOR: In one sense I am starting to agree with you. Your skua has become a gull.

AMG: Actually, the more I see, the more I am convinced that juvenile Long-taileds have the body of a skua but the mind of a Kittiwake. Except when high winds force them down and into wave troughs, they are content simply to tootle along, often several metres above the sea, and frequently stall, hover and swoop down to check for food on the surface. Also, when patrolling in the air, they are strangely reluctant to settle for more than a few seconds. No sooner have they plopped down than they are up again: it is as though the water was a hot bath and they were nearly scalded. Killian Mullarney gave me that tip.

EDITOR: At last, a bit of gen from a more reliable observer. Has he any illustrations? Could you have a word with him and get back to me? Tell him that *Birdwatch* would like to publish his artwork and, if he has any original thoughts on the matter, we would put those in print too. Goodnight.

August 1994
Birdwatch

Heir
line

The heirs went back to school this morning after two riotous months free of confinement and, thanks to some heavy-handed role reversal, I've been their keeper all summer. As a former child myself, I kind of enjoyed the Mrs Doubtfire experience, although I won't be disclosing that fact to their mother. She thinks my ease with the kids is because I've read up on child psychology and in a way, I suppose she's right. The technique is called selective ignorance. Never put kids under surveillance as it can frighten you and lead to personal injury through panic-stricken rushes to the scene of innocent screams and harmless crashes.

Trying to predict their jizz is equally futile. This year's costly presents from a Canadian trip were ignored in favour of tree-growing kits that I picked up free. In a box about half the size of a McDonald's Happy Meal, you get a small bag of peat, a handful of seeds and a page of basic instructions. To a kid the text: 'carefully add a little water to the peat', immediately sets off a chain reaction of spoons, trowels, extra compost and eventually widespread flooding. The upshot is an even greater problem, for the seeds they planted all germinated and the craze has swept the street. Whole flocks of kids are sowing apple and orange pips in garden sandpits and expecting similar results. This has displaced Power Ranger battles from outdoor arenas and brought them back indoors, thereby endangering household infrastructure and heirlooms. I'm dreading being fingered as the culprit. The last thing I want is eco-wars with the neighbours.

By 11 o'clock, I had just started into the housework (amassing major credits for October - to hell with principles, a man's got to live), when in through the front door bursts Cute Cafolla, one of birding's new generation. This guy doesn't look more than 17 and is knee-high to a snake, but has a Mediterranean complexion with a very homely kisser that always has a big Ovaltine smile. He is without doubt as good-looking as any bloke has a right to be without arousing suspicion. However, I can see instantly that he has not called to help with the vacuuming. In fact, he is so hot and flustered that you could probably fry an egg on any part of him.

I say, "What's the news, Cute? Go ahead, spit it out." "I reckon I've seen an Ortolan Bunting in the big stubble field at Kearney. I got a pretty good look at it but it flew and I lost it somewhere

Being on your own when faced with the identification of a cryptic bunting can be a tough challenge for a young birder.

in the field. I'm sure it's still there." Oh boy. Over here Ortolan Bunting is big potatoes. I could see that he needed to be sure that I believed him, for if there is anything a young guy hates it is an older guy doubting his ability. "Cute, if you're looking for a bloodhound to go look for this, then you've got one. Come on." I whipped off the apron and we jumped in his car, which was as neat as a new pin, maybe neater. On the way he relived the morning's excitement. He'd flushed the bird out of short grass, seen it pitch in and had an agonizing time trying to scope it but through sheer persistence he'd clinched it on eye-ring, pinkish bill and fine streaking down the side of the chest. This was a lifer for him and he was trembling, either from the thrill of finding it or the worry that we might not relocate it. I knew exactly how he felt: I've been that soldier.

We went straight to the spot where he last saw it, drew a blank, quartered the field together and then split up, him thrashing the rough cover along a fence-line, me the short turf near the shore. That's where it was, sneaking along the side of a path. When Cute arrived at my side his blood pressure was up in the paint cards and might have peaked at a full coronary if I'd told him there and then what we were really looking at – which was a Lapland Bunting.

How was he going to react to this proposition? I knew he didn't want to start his career by becoming the greatest stringer since the invention of the seine net, so I decided to talk him through the identification nice and slowly, and let him discover the inescapable conclusion for himself. I said, "Well, you were right about the eye-ring and bill colour, although only the base of the bill is really pink. Plus, the middle of the chest is unstreaked." He agreed. So far so good. Now for the tricky bit. "Cute, the amount

of rufous in the tertials and especially that panel across the greater coverts is a big problem. Only Lapland Bunting shows such bright rufous, although Ortolans can appear quite similar towards sunset." That last bit isn't true of course – I only said it in a paternal capacity.

It's hard to escape the sense of responsibility that parenthood brings. I felt concerned for Cute, anxious for him not to be annoyed by his mistake but rather to see it in a positive light: that mistakes are a necessary part of everyone's learning process, young and old alike. We stood for a while and talked a little more about the finer points of bunting identification. Finally, I summoned up the strength to say it. "So, Cute, I hope you're not too disappointed that this is only a Lapland Bunting." Cute Cafolla got out of this situation with such dexterity that would have pleased Harry Houdini. "No way," he said, "that makes it two ticks in one morning."

November 1996
Birdwatch

Sea-dog
days

Ideas are like mercury in the bloodstream. Once they get into your system you are stuck with them. In 1982 I read a wonderful account – Voyage for a Life-Lister – by Frank Graham Jr in *Audubon* that described a two-day birdwatching trip on a fast boat chartered to visit the edge of the continental shelf 160 miles southeast of Gloucester, Massachusetts. Thirty-five birders were on board, many were seasick, the sea was rough, and conditions were gruelling. "The handrails at which we clutched were cold and wet, so that after we had been on deck all morning the flesh of our fingers took on the pallid-blue doughiness of a corpse that had been awash for a day or two." But, armed with chum, they found a White-faced Storm Petrel. A sensational result. Think about it. I'm an Irish birder surrounded by ocean – life would not have a point unless I knew what was over the horizon. In terms of personal development, the article might equally well have been entitled How To Make an Atomic Bomb. It talked about chum ingredients, the target-rich environment of the continental shelf, and even the drugs to be used to prevent seasickness. I was married with a career – a good time to try something different. Why, even the term for such seafaring sorties was new and exciting. The Yanks called them 'pelagic trips'. I opened the dictionary. 'Pelagic: of, inhabiting, or carried out in, the deep sea or ocean.' "Darling,"

I said, "I might try my hand at organizing a birdwatching boat trip." "That sounds lovely," she said, "is it a kind of cruise that I could go on too?"

The first pelagic was easy to organize. My boss was fascinated by all things nautical and coming close to retirement, had invested in a big boy's toy. It was also something of a geriatric – an old, slow boat. It had been a Scottish trawler and although it put-putted along at not much more than jogging pace it still retained a drunken Rab C Nesbitt roll that quickly separated future pelagic stalwarts from towel-hugging blobs of misery. In many ways that maiden voyage qualified only as a pelagic lite. While we may have tracked North by Northwest (into seas off north Donegal) the trip was no Hitchcock thriller. We were never out of sight of land, everybody had a bunk, and the crew even fed us. Hardly heroic. We tried fish guts as chum but the big bits blocked the barrel. Then, when confronted with clouds of feeding Stormies (European Storm Petrels), we felt that it might be impossible to pick out a Wilson's Storm Petrel. In those days, we were greenhorns and so were the field-guides.

Time to aim higher. I wanted to try and reach the edge of the continental shelf, to take a boat off southwest Ireland (closer

to the edge of the theoretical range of Wilson's), and to be out of sight of land. We speculated that true pelagic species would always avoid the coast. Once they clocked it, they would steer back out to sea – which was why we never saw dreambirds such as Fea's Petrels from headlands. Furthermore, we conjectured that mythical vagrants – Little Shearwater, for example – might even prove to be regular among the huge feeding rafts of Manx Shearwaters that tantalized us in the retina-straining 'Sabinosphere' at the limit of telescope vision. There is always one. Someone who asks the question that you never saw coming. "Anthony, I'm a bit concerned. If we see Wilson's and it is 50 miles out, can I count it on my Irish List? Will I be outside the ticking zone?" Despite that comment, we brought him along – but only as emergency chum.

We needed a new boat. If theories were going to be tested, the vessel would have to depart from west Cork – the diametrically opposite end of the country from where I lived. In those pre-Google days I had no means of acquiring contacts so I did the next-best thing: I asked my mother if her worldwide web of religious links might turn up trumps. Surely there must be the odd shark-fishing bishop? She organized an appeal on Irish radio, broadcast by no less than Gay Byrne, the nation's favourite radio and television presenter. It worked. Of several replies, I liked most the sound of a young trawler skipper from Castletownbere on the very edge of southwest Cork. He would do the trip but it would be entirely at our risk. I enquired about how many the boat could take. "Legally?" he asked. "Not necessarily," I replied. There was a pause. "Legally, none. But there are six bunks." I said, "How does 25 sound? These guys are desperate. They will sleep in the fish hold if it comes to that."

He said some would have to. However, he would hose it down beforehand. My kind of guy!

That summer I drove down to meet him and more importantly, check out the boat. It was ideal. A high front, access to all sides behind a tall guardrail and a wide, open back for dispensing chum and getting unobstructed close-up photographs (ha-ha). We agreed a departure date for a two-day trip – 17 August 1985 – and I triggered the largest-ever carbon footprint in the history of Irish birding. Friends flew from England; a fleet of hire cars was chartered – mainly to transport a phenomenal 80 gallons of chum – and the chum itself had been mixed into a puree with the aid of a cement mixer. By the time the posse swept into town at close to midnight (the agreed sailing time) the mood was comparable to astronauts preparing for a moon-shot. Alas, there was no sign of the skipper. At least our ship was in the harbour. However, two things sounded alarm bells. First, the boat had been freshly painted and all the woodwork was sticky. Second, 'she' was called *Piranha*. Assuming a nonchalant pastoral air, I pretended that I knew where to find the skipper and told everyone to make themselves at home, sweep rats out of bunks, and get some sleep.

Meanwhile, I tried to calm down. I expected to locate the ship's master in the nearest pub. If not, the locals would know where he hung out. They did. He was in Allihes, twelve miles away over the mountains. I drove there. At least there was only one pub to search. He wasn't in it. In growing desperation, I asked the barman if he knew where he drank. "Eddie Sheedy is it? He's out the back." That is where I found him. He hardly knew me. He was drunk and his hands were blue. I recognized the

For some reason my proposal - that it was time to consider pelagic trips - fell on deaf ears. Inset: Sabine's Gull.

127

shade right away. It was the colour he had just painted his trawler, the sky blue of Cambridge in the boat race. Later, it became known as *Piranha* blue. I didn't know what to say. He spoke first, "Jesus, you are early – let me get you a pint." Panic over.

It was 0300hrs by the time he arrived. The estimated value of the trawler was at least a quarter of a million pounds, which made it the most expensive craft that I have ever driven – or steered, to be more precise. Despite the Guinness, he was sublime at turning the boat around and then heading her out into the Atlantic. That didn't take long and, assuming that on a clear night we shouldn't hit anything, he left me at the wheel with fewer instructions than you receive when taking a seat in a dodgem.

He didn't reappear at the controls until, with the boat slobbering and lurching in deep swells in early morning, a wave the size of a bank statement jolted us hard enough to tip him out of his bunk and onto the floor. He burst into the cabin and regained command. He looked at the big navigation screen to see where we were (35 miles west of Fastnet) and went off to boil the kettle. When he returned I gave him a summary of what we had seen so far. That was when I realised that our interests were poles apart – birds versus money. A more important objective was to convince him that we were at least human even if we weren't, in his eyes, 'normal'. He had a wife, but seemed to be a single man at heart. He wasn't quite in love with the sea either; he regarded it more as a place of refuge. That was enough for a man. Over the course of our exchanges I felt the beginnings of a rapport, which I cemented by using plenty of bad language, berating the

activities of foreign fishing fleets and sounding – even smelling – like a hard-drinking man.

With daylight fully established, the growing number of seabirds constantly distracted me. Gannets, Fulmars, Bonxies and Stormies were regular. And, yes, there was the first Great Shearwater skimming across the bow. That had the desired effect – it woke everybody up and facilitated a head count. Each of the 25 revellers who had elbowed their way on board in the dark was still here. Over the next eight hours we tried hard to sieve for surprises. The day deteriorated, becoming grey and increasingly windy. Cheer and expectation drained from ruddy faces that had been vibrant the day before. Periodically, the boat cut engines and drifted with chum slicks. Retching became the only human sound. People's power of concentration waned at the constant effort of compensating for the pitching of the boat by holding binoculars with one hand and clutching a rail with the other. By mid-afternoon the weather closed in, birds disappeared, and spirits hit rock bottom. A council of war was convened, which voted for an early return to port – still 50 miles over the horizon. Those who were too sick to vote were assumed to be in favour. This had become the *Marie Celeste* of pelagics. In fact, apart from Killian Mullarney, there was no-one left on deck who was still capable, awake, or remotely interested in watching for birds.

Then the Almighty clicked his fingers. Killian hissed at me, "Quick, get on that petrel." What petrel, where? There was no means of predicting its movements, no chance to turn the boat or pour chum. Killian was frantic but his gaze was increasingly astern – the opposite direction to the boat's path. Time did that thing where it slows to a crawl. Then, in answer to something,

Revel in the birds you see; don't wallow in the misery of those you miss (and vice versa).
Schadenfreude and pelagic trips go together like peaches and sour cream.

Wilson's Storm Petrel

it reappeared, rode an air pocket in the lee of a wall of sea and vanished into a trough. "Wilson's!" We had seen enough to be sure. The frosty carpal bar, broad 'thin as paper' wings, all-dark underwings, and sticklike dangling legs. Sweet Mother of God, this was it – the first live Wilson's seen off Ireland.

Pandemonium ensued. The dead walked, hearts burst, and life-lists went into suspended animation as their owners fought desperately to wring a glimpse of heaven from among a forest of moving waves. More chum – the special barrel with Lourdes water added – was dumped overboard and there, at last, was the phantom. The bird could not have been more obliging nor

its watchers more satisfied. The full effects of its mighty blow would be felt forever. For months afterwards, flecks of *Piranha* blue on binoculars and clothing were cherished until they flaked off. Everyone was amazed at the bird's distinctiveness, yet one of the sharpest observers was Eddie. He rose to the occasion and reversed the boat back and forth over the chum slick, picking out the quarry with a naked eye from the dozens of Stormies. Pelagics are a truly communal experience – and that includes the skipper.

August trips with Eddie became an annual thing for a time. The status of Wilson's Storm Petrel was rewritten but bigger scores did not come our way. Time for a change of scene. The World Series of Birding, held each May in New Jersey, became the other big annual event around which my world turned. To fit in all the pre-race scouting and then the Big Day itself, the team – to begin with, Mark, Bruce, Killian and myself – allocated a fortnight in America. You would think that, after a knackering 24-hour bird race, nobody would be able for much more. Not Constantine. He went for my Achilles' heel. After the race, would I try and set up a pelagic off North Carolina – out to the Gulf Stream to look for Black-capped Petrels, Bridled Terns, South Polar Skuas and who-knows-what-else? I wondered where he got the idea until I heard the words to a tune that he liked to hum. The artist was Warren Zevon, the song 'I'll sleep when I'm dead'. We decided to go for it.

Letters were written, contacts made, and we were to rendezvous with our fixer, Bob Ake, at Cape Hatteras the night before the trip. After a very long drive we were late. Instead of arriving in time for dinner, we got there in time for breakfast. Bob was worried. Not about us. He told us we could sleep during the two hours it took for the speedboat to reach the edge of the Gulf Stream. Unlike Irish pelagics, we were headed for a hotspot so well defined that you could even see a change in sea colour and feel a difference in water temperature. Blue ocean collided with green Gulf Stream and created a ribbon of richness along which a seabird conveyor-belt operated. But there was a problem. Weather? No. Mechanical problems with the boat? No. What then? Bob's regular skipper wasn't available and we had to find someone else. The guy who Bob had in mind was dithering. Apparently, he was, ahem, concerned about his reputation. Hello?

To 'understand', we needed a lesson in American machismo. Each dawn, an armada of gleaming white sports boats zooms out to the Gulf Stream after tuna and sailfish. The big sailfish are not landed. If hooked, they are played for sport and then released. In other words, this is Big Game hunting where you don't kill the animals; you just annoy the hell out of them. Skippers vie with each other and brag about their catch at the end of the day. We, of course, would be coming back empty-handed. That was not so much bad for business – it was bad for image. At the time we were oblivious to the reasons for the impasse. We stood on the dock while Bob did the talking. The skipper's dog wandered up to sniff the strangers and Rover and Bruce seemed to hit it off big time. Pretty soon it was like a scene from *Lassie Come Home*. Bob bounced up and said we were going. Only later did the penny drop. The dog got us the trip.

The boat was amazing. It was a rocket-powered gin palace. We could try out the accoutrements if we liked – sit in the barbershop 'fighting chairs' with legs uncrossed to accommodate the big socket where the butt end of seven-foot-long fibreglass poles slotted between our legs, help ourselves to snacks and cold drinks or, as we all did, snooze on the white leather settees. As if the contrast to *Piranha* was not dramatic enough, I noted how speed and the absence of a trawler's roll, negated queasiness. I marvelled at the deep cobalt of the water and also the fact that, birding in intense overhead sunlight, sunglasses were essential to see birds against a shiny sea that glistened like tinfoil. There was a shout of "Okay, y'awl?" and the roar of the engines subsided to a gentle purr. Clearly, we had arrived. We were at a place where the ocean turned from abyssal blue to a perfect grass green, as though you had been watering the lawn and didn't stop and now the back garden is a hundred fathoms deep.

Great Shearwater

It was a species I knew but almost did not recognize. The birds looked different; their cumulus cloud white underwings and bellies flashed and made them look like terns against an inky sea. Yet, the grace and poise was unmistakeable. They were Cory's Shearwaters. Hold on a minute. What's that? A Great Shearwater – nice for me but manna for Mark. His long-awaited first. What a fantastic start! Why couldn't Irish pelagics be like this? Then, as you do, a worry shot through my head. I hoped we hadn't peaked too soon. Bob was beside me and I told him that if the day continued like this we would be hysterically happy. What followed was a piece of information that, although not classified, was explosive. He said that, if we wished, we could remain with the flock of Cory's and a few Greats all day. The boat had the power to keep up with them. He recommended that. His reason was not just so Mark could watch his Holy Grail until he felt sick, it was because the flock would attract other birds. And – Eureka! – he was right. One Great Shearwater seemed like it was going bald, which left a big black eye to dominate its face. In the course of the next second I went from bemused to ballistic. It wasn't a Great Shearwater – idiot! – it was a Black-capped Petrel. Eventually a dozen more joined the growing cast of big shearwaters.

Mark asked me how I was feeling. My blood pressure was probably unreadable due to the anticipation. He wondered if I sensed the emotions Ross and Sabine must have experienced when they looked open-mouthed at new birds in strange lands. "Not really," I said, "I'd like to think Don Johnson and *Miami Vice* might be a better analogy." It was that kind of trip – a petrol-head pelagic. The skipper had positioned us at the epicentre of the first cloud of birds he had seen. Having done his bit, we were into combat immediately. I focussed on a wheeling group of dark birds. I didn't know what was going to fill my binoculars – immature Gannets? We had flushed several off the sea on the way out. For a moment I couldn't believe what I was looking at.

Did we bring chum? "Yes," Bob said. He fished out a Tupperware box and a soup ladle. My eyes were on stalks. "Is that it?" I said. "Why, how much do you Irish guys bring?" he replied. I didn't tell him in case he reported me to Greenpeace. He dribbled the elixir onto the surface. Drop by drop it expanded into a smelly serpentine rainbow, spilling downwind of us. Like Eddie, the skipper was very attentive. However, today's ship's master was only concerned that Bob didn't spill any on the pristine deck. The shearwater entourage was not that bothered at the appearance of the unexpected oily treat. We anticipated that. We had other fish to fry. Soon the first Wilson's appeared. It was weird to see them on their own, without the identification challenge. What else might be drawn to the fray? I knew what was at the back of Bob's mind but to avoid a jinx, I didn't want to say its name. Off Ireland, its sister species usually quickly drops from the sky once chum is decanted and there is a captive audience to beat up. Would the same happen here? It was ridiculous to sit in a white leather seat with ice-cold coke in a cup-holder watching Wilson's Storm Petrels in luxury and still expect more. But you know what birders are like. Out here, waiting and hoping could never be in vain. Both Sooty and Bridled Terns drifted by and an Audubon's Shearwater was nominated for an Oscar when it dip-fed over the sea like a large pied storm petrel. Years later, I saw a Little Shearwater do the same thing off Tenerife.

It was hard to resist the temptation to declare a siesta. With virtually no sleep for three days, the gentle rocking and warm sun was having a soporific effect. Even the butterfly fluttering of the Wilson's was starting to relax eyelids and make them want to droop. Then, in an instant, the ballerina chorus of Wilson's broke ranks and scattered. Snoozing Cory's awoke with a start and lumbered into flight, taxiing down the valleys between the waves. Something had panicked the birds. Off Ireland, I would be looking for a Great Black-backed Gull, Grey Seal, or maybe a pod of Bottle-nosed Dolphins. What constituted a villain off North Carolina? Frigatebird, Marlin, or Moby Dick? What appeared was better than any of those. A South Polar Skua. Having migrated north from breeding grounds clustered around the Antarctic Peninsula to enjoy a summer holiday off the east coast of the United States, it was in a pretty relaxed mood. Short of hand-

feeding it, we could not have had better views. Surely, we couldn't top that? The truth is, we didn't plan to.

The finale to the trip happened utterly accidentally. The captain was beginning to open up his 212-horsepower diesel engine and head for home. For kicks, we were joy-riding among some Sooty Shearwaters. Bruce, a polite Canadian and phlegmatic as a hibernating Grizzly, suddenly shouted. Hollered, more like. "What is that?" I looked at the Sooty Shearwater look-alike. It was boomeranging around in flight with pale blotches permeating dark belly plumage and a messy white band on its underwings. By a process of elimination – start by thinking deliciously rare – the only possibility seemed to be a dark morph Herald Petrel. The next command was mine: "Skipper, follow that petrel!" We bounded after it, snapping blurry photographs as we went. The chase was manic since the quarry was not a mere shearwater; it was a gadfly-petrel, the greatest freewheeling seabird genus in the Solar System. At last my *Piranha* experience came in handy. I stood astride wheel and captain and kept his eye on the bird. It was the devil to follow and jinked and swerved at random. At times he missed its feints and I had to grab the wheel to keep a bead on it. It was madcap stuff but we saw it well and perhaps more importantly, considering it was the first live record for North America, we got some pictures.

The voyage became the trip of legends. Even Bob Ake got a lifer. He couldn't stop smiling. I assumed the Herald Petrel was his personal highlight of the day, if not ever? Wrong. He said, "Anthony, what you did with this guy's boat was like going up to the British Monarch, lifting the crown off her head, and trying it on for size. Birders one, macho mariners nil." I was shocked. I never meant to 'upstage' him. Should I apologise? Bob said, "No, don't do that. He thinks you are a bunch of namby-pambies, so he's not bothered." Still, I thought I should at least have a quiet chat with him as we motored back to Hatteras. I told him a little about boat trips I'd made off Ireland and complimented him on his beautiful boat. She was thirty-four-foot long, he told me. "Why, that's amazing," I said. "The lifeboat we keep on *Piranha* is exactly the same size!"

Over the next few years I was happy to look back on the Great Pelagic Push and started to regard it like an old romance. No major-league birders younger than me showed any sign of 'pioneering'. All except one. Martin Garner has a way of asking questions that, when he is finished, leaves you feeling pummelled and confused like a groggy prizefighter. However, as with all good interrogators, he leaves a lifeline in case you want to redeem yourself. This time, in front of witnesses, he seized upon the fact that - since the glory days of the 1980s - the tide had well and truly ebbed on Irish seabird trips. He wanted to know why. I gave him several reasons. Probably the most important was the lack of lifers once people bagged a Wilson's. Why, some trips were even abandoned the second a Wilson's was ticked-off. He was aghast. I said, "It's as if everyone has grown apathetic and mercenary. They believe they aren't going to see anything rare, so they are done with pioneering." That did it. He had me on a hook that I couldn't wriggle off. I backtracked. Well, yes, I would still like to try. The probing continued. "The basic problem," I said sharply, "is finding a decent boat and a sympathetic owner." I mentioned Eddie, his leaky boat with just one lifejacket, and the nature of the crew - us. "It was like putting Saint Trinian's in charge of *Titanic*."

The witnesses, my younger brother and 10-year-old son, took their cue. "Come on dad. Don't be such a big wimp. You could sort out a boat for us." They could see it all. The quick phone-call to a bird tour company to book places on an air-conditioned cruiser, the calm aquamarine sea, masses of tubenoses endlessly circling the ship, and an onboard McDonald's serving Happy Meals. Martin had been dealt an ace. He'd managed to get my next-of-kin on his side. I said, "What do you think I am – crazy? I may have had a screw or two loose in the past but at the moment everything is just about bolted together and that's the way I intend to keep it. No chance." This was my way of adding drama to the trip, for Martin had inadvertently rekindled an old idea. Why not try a voyage off Donegal, closer to home?

I phoned the fish processors at Burtonport, the preferred point of departure, and got the grim news that the district's trawlers had been mothballed. Economics favoured the battleship-sized hulks operating out of Killybegs. Unless I fancied contacting Neil Gallagher, a local who did inshore angling charters? I tried Killybegs. There, at the fishing cooperative, I talked to the Man Who Knows Everything. Before I had even finished speaking, this gargoyle told me that fishermen had better things to do with their weekends than take a crowd of nancy-boys out birdwatching; if we wanted to see seagulls there was plenty flying around Killybegs harbour. How do you deal with animosity on that level? Quite simple. I said, "Thanks for the advice. It looks like the people I really need to speak to are the Dutch, who seem to be the only nation brave enough to operate on the edge of Ireland's continental shelf." Click. In desperation I rang Neil Gallagher. What kind of charters did he do? He was prepared to go 30 miles out and had a boat that went like a Messerschmitt. He even supplied chum. Bingo! As ever, there was a caveat.

Everything hinged on the weather. In reality, it depended on his wife's meteorological skills. She would be Queen Solomon for, while he is at sea, she scrutinizes marine bulletins. I should contact her for a green light. Mrs Gallagher knew more about forecasts than I did – horoscope forecasts, that is. The woman confused anticyclones with uncles and cousins. My wife, who reads this stuff in draft to keep me out of court, says that last line was "just like a man". Mrs McGeehan hoped that girl power would triumph and that the trip would be cancelled, thereby sparing our son (you know what women are like).

Although I will never know for sure, I suspect that my mother was commissioned to pray for fine weather. A miraculous ridge of high pressure descended on our date. At the quayside the astonishing happenings continued – the skipper was sober and ready to go. Neil was a paragon of organization and seemed as keen as we were. Eagerness is always palpable at the start of a pelagic. Participants are wannabe explorers, about to boldly go and conquer uncharted ornithological waters. By lunchtime the mood was mutinous. The sea was dead. Even the chum was ignored. It was diet chum. Folk took on a look of resignation tinged with despair. Some seemed to be awaiting the services of a taxidermist. No Wilson's. Not even a 'crummy' Sabine's Gull. We badly needed action before most slipped into a persistent vegetative state. Trying to muster a show of unquenchable optimism, I directed Neil to intercept a lone seabird and alerted all souls to get ready as the target glided past. I had noticed a cap and a patterned back. The odds favoured Great Shearwater, our first of the day at last. I didn't realise it at the time, but I had put us on a collision course with nirvana. Everybody crowded at the rail. The bird was going to pass in full sun. And there it was. It swept up into the air and straight into the record books.

Fea's Petrel

It wasn't a Great Shearwater – it was the first Fea's Petrel to be seen on a pelagic off Britain or Ireland. Alas, it never stopped. Pursuit was fruitless. But memories are priceless. An erstwhile ghost ship had been transformed. Sometimes birders forget to look hard when they forget what it feels like to find something good.

May 2008

Constructive
criticism

Mrs McGeehan *addresses the state of the union*

It's always a temptation to second-guess a marriage and say where it went wrong but it's been my philosophy not to kick a man when he's down and that goes for Anthony, although it would be easy to fault him. Up to now I've turned a blind eye while he's led a fairytale life in this column, chewing the fat with all you fellow braves, even though it's left to me to feed him ideas, check his grammar and – basically – put up with the bozo. So the recent trouble started, not because he uses me as a personal guinea pig to fuel his limited powers of literary invention, but because he cast himself in a role for above his station in life.

In a recent gospel (Birding from the Hip, November 1996) I read with increasing incredulity that he now attributes Mrs Doubtfire qualities to himself right down to wearing a pinny ("I whipped off the apron": his exact words). He's supposed to have looked after the kids, done chores and even used the vacuum cleaner. Well, the last time he used that was to get some dirt out of his telescope and, when it comes to dusting and ironing, he moves at a pace slower than the speed of Dutch elm disease. The crunch came last month when he went into print with, "Birding from the Hip is 50 today." And then what? Not only was there no

mention of the three columns that I wrote, but also it's pretty obvious that he is crediting them to himself. I wonder, would he be so quick to steal my sciatica?

For women, it's easy to worry and feel guilty about letting others down, behaving selfishly and not showing compassion. We shouldn't. These were the very nerves I was keen to touch when I confronted my husband with what he'd done. It was after supper and he was giving off about groups such as the Spice Girls who don't write their own material. He was filled with that happy sense of purpose people have when they are standing up for a principle they haven't been knocked down for yet. When I told him that he was guilty of doing the same thing, he turned bright red just like the inflammation on a baboon's hinder. Then I swooped and said, "In my book that makes you a phoney, a plagiarist and, worst of all, a useless dnegaf - a man of straw." That last line really got him going. When it comes to words, he regards himself as a kind of educated buff, but he relaxed when I told him that 'dnegaf' was only fag end spelled backwards. I didn't mention that the same rule applied to "man of 'straw'". Next morning, there was no sign of him.

Unless Ireland's first Green Woodpecker is also clamped against this tree, he is going to surprise me!

What is it that makes a seemingly properly adjusted male of the species rise from a warm bed on a Sunday morning, don a manure-encrusted woolly hat and set out into a cold and miserable dawn? From the time of Shakespeare, long-suffering wives have bemoaned this behaviour: "She laments – her husband goes this morning a-birding," *Merry Wives of Windsor*. Even Mrs Audubon "regarded every bird as a rival."

But is there an alternative explanation? Is he really seeing another woman? If so, would he be capable? Let's look at the evidence. On weekdays it takes a gallon of tea to wake Anthony up. He can scarcely dress himself, never mind the kids, and he is so disorganized that an encyclopaedia of post-its is required to remind him of what he has to do. Yet, come Sunday, he springs out of bed, finds time to shave, shower, make a lunch, remembers waterproofs, gloves, wellies, extra socks, binoculars, telescope, tripod, camera, money, teabags and flask – right down to spoon and collapsible umbrella (the big sissy).

There is the veil of secrecy about his whereabouts. He never takes me to see where he goes and, when I ask him where he's been, he always comes out with the same cloak-and-dagger reply: "St John's." It transpires that this covers all three of his regular haunts: St John's Point, County Down; St John's Point, County Donegal; and St John's, Newfoundland, Canada! It has just occurred to me that if he didn't show up some evening and I had to call the police because I was worried he'd had an accident, I wouldn't know which St. John's to direct them to. Mind you, there could be certain advantages here.

Cue the acid test. At the moment it is one o'clock in the morning. So far, I have spent half an hour on this letter and now my spouse,

his greying Richard Gere locks, Romeo eyes and athletic frame clad only in a white silk sheet, rolls against me and says, "Quit writing to your girlfriends and let's play doctors and nurses." If only. Instead he plonks his big cold feet on my legs, which has about the same electrifying effect as a cattle prod. Something is bothering him. I run my fingers through his hair and ask, "What's up honey; can I help?"

Well, I couldn't. Late yesterday afternoon he found a bird that was either a Common Sandpiper or – big news, apparently – a Spotted Sandpiper. He is at his wit's end because he cannot decide which. You'll like this next bit. In the midst of his babbling, I suddenly became aware that he was actually talking about breast plumage and saying things such as, "Young Spotted Sandpipers have plunging breast-lines, somehow different from Common Sandpiper." I said, "Would a Spotted Sandpiper's pattern remind you of cleavage?" "PRECISELY!" he exclaimed.

Well that was it. He was out of bed in a flash and off to consult his bird books. Eight years into a marriage and I appear to be stuck with a man who pays more attention to avian anatomy than mine. I guess I needn't have worried about him catching the seven-year-itch. However, he seems oblivious to the fact that, thanks (or is it no thanks?) to him, I'm on the verge of succumbing to the eight-year rash.

February 1997
Birdwatch

Is **this** it?

Next to 'team building' the words 'global warming' have become my bête noire. I am fed up with hearing that soon the polar ice caps are going to be something small enough to drop into a G&T or that I might help save the Earth by taking the groceries home in a 'bag for life' and thereby prevent the Eskimos from waking up in a puddle. It is good that *almost* collectively (this means you, George W Bush) the human race is indulging in a bout of international soul-searching over the mess that we have made of this planet. However, we might be on the cusp of witnessing a final irony. Mother Nature could have the last laugh as we accelerate the natural process of grinding ourselves to dust. Instead of living within our means and enjoying this beautiful world, we have crapped in our own nest.

Listening to the debates – is climate change occurring as part of a natural rhythm or has it been triggered by people – the thread shared by both sides is a need to address the consequences of the situation *for the benefit of man.* I don't detect much of a hymn for conservation. Instead of 'scrap the motor car,' read 'we need bio-fuels to replace petrol.' No root-and-branch lifestyle change there. It reminded me of what Einstein said when asked about the kind of weaponry with which World War III would be waged. "I cannot tell you that," he said. But he knew what World War IV would be fought with – sticks and stones.

Apart from fish, is there anyone around who is looking forward to rising sea levels? Do national stereotypes reveal different attitudes? No better race to ask than the Dutch. Living below sea level already, how much more can they take before preparing breakfast becomes hand-to-hand combat with seals? Being creative types, the Dutch plan to raise dike defences on a vast scale and protect the country by pumping sand from the bed of the North Sea to create a new battlement peninsula running north from The Hague. In England, plans to protect London include, in the first instance, raising the Thames barrier. If that fails, Plan B is the time-honoured formula of annexing Scotland and running the show from dry land in Edinburgh. In Ireland, worries about the future are centred on the moral corruption of Irish youth who, it is feared, will take to the beaches in the heat-wave climate and turn to a life of bikinis and debauchery.

Perhaps I was knocking on the wrong door. What about Newfoundland? A cold, snowy wilderness frequently shrouded in fog when the temperatures tip above freezing. "Are you worried about retreating glaciers?" I asked a local resident. "They cannot retreat fast enough," he said. His biggest worry was that, if the weather warmed, he would have to spend money on a fridge to keep beer chilled. So it's true, it is hard to disobey the selfish gene with which we were born. In millennia to come, man's likely disappearance from the face of the Earth will be

"If you bump into Jesus, do you think he could help us out?"

lamented as much as the departure of ear-to-ear acne from the face of a teenage girl.

I stumbled across a statistic recently that walloped me over the head and left me reeling. Ageing of Bowhead Whales reveals that the species is exceptionally long-lived, easily passing 100 years of age. One recently dead male was 211. As the American researcher commented, that means the animal's life spanned the presidencies of both Thomas Jefferson and Bill Clinton. A blip measured against evolutionary time but think of the changes wrought by western man's guns, God and germs in the same two centuries. I am a bit leery about including God in that company. As my mother always says, God has a plan for us. Actually, I quite liked the first part of his plan, as enunciated in The Book of Genesis, "On the fifth day God said, 'Let the waters bring forth swarms of living creatures, and let the birds fly above the Earth. So God created every winged bird according to its kind. And God blessed them by saying, 'Be fruitful and multiply.'" So there you have it, underneath his mouldering exterior, God is a manic splitter. So maybe global warming is 'his' way of booting avian evolution up the backside.

But what about us? We might not be around to tick off all the new species. Finally, the Brits would get those endemic species that they have tried so hard to string. Forget Red Grouse and Scottish Crossbill. Thanks to rising sea levels, Britain would literally become 'little old England', a remote island outcrop where endemism and speciation would occur on a scale rivalling the Galapagos. Within a handful of millennia, evolution and an underground *British Ornithologists Union* would have created Flightless Canada Goose, Pennine Accentor, Three-barred Crossbill and, of course, British Rail.

Writing these wannabe prophetic words I am beginning to feel as though I have been made the captain of the Titanic an hour after hitting the iceberg and am sensing the ship start to slide under. I have to write fast – cough up each idea as though it were a salmon bone stuck in my oesophagus. So, in watching birds lies our best hope of survival. They are role models. We need to heed their lessons. Descended from dinosaurs, they have come a long way. Mum could be right, it might be pre-ordained that the subsequent development of the human race will follow that of birds.

Will we sprout wings? Of course not, but we may be in for an evolutionary 'correction'. There are already signs of it. Increasingly, male members of the human race seem to be in closer touch with their feminine side. Just look at David Beckham. Earrings, a ponytail and a rigorous daily regime of moisturizing, are the hallmarks of the modern male. Boys no longer charge about with toy guns playing cowboys and Indians. The sperm-count is in sharp decline. Men are going the way of male birds. Testicles are evolving into gonads, seasonally active sex organs that shrivel to the size of a raisin after their annual outing. Testosterone will become extinct and be replaced with a benign chemical similar to Nivea For Men. Society will be matriarchal, just like birds. The planet will be saved as a Feminine Reich replaces the plundering of natural resources fuelled by machismo. Personally, womankind cannot take over the world quick enough for me. The best may be yet to come.

November 2008

Fowl
play

I hesitate, but not for long, to mention a knotty little personal problem that I'm not supposed to talk about. Anyone who has the albatross around their neck of writing a monthly column will sympathize. The difficulty is this: today is Thursday, the first day of April, and by tomorrow night I'm supposed to be on a plane to Texas. Lucky old me.

But hold on a minute. Before I go, I've got a kitchen to paint, a tumbledrier to mend and an epistle of 1,000 honeyed words to scribe, otherwise Dominic Mitchell will have me kneecapped for breach of contract. I'm stuck for a subject to write about. Humour, my preferred genre, is fine as a weapon for poking fun at things stuck in birding's alimentary canal – such as Ireland's flocks of Lesser Short-toed Larks – but this morning I am torn between literature's muse and matrimony's survival training.

I thought about a little homily on the Blue Tit couple that are busy nest-building next door. My neighbour, a retired professional lady, rushed up to me recently in Tesco's and announced in front of onlookers that her tits had come back. She is in Australia until the end of next month so her car hasn't moved much of late: especially the exhaust's tail pipe, which caught the eye of the birds. I know that, when children are born, it is customary to say that they have been 'launched into the big wide world'. A phrase the Blue Tit kids could soon experience literally. Eureka! There's my theme - humanity and birds.

Have you ever noticed that, often times, people are much nicer to birds than they are to each other? The same unnamed folk who spontaneously develop a bad back at the mention of needing a helping hand to erect a garden fence, are transformed into good Samaritans when birds are in trouble. Take last August, when Ards distillery leaked alcohol into a stream that emptied onto the mudflats of Strangford Lough. Many fish became intoxicated and floated to the surface, providing easy pickings for dozens of plunge-diving Common Terns. Unfortunately, the terns' happy hour was short-lived and they too began to keel over. A public outcry ensued and poisoning was suspected. Luckily for the birds the effects of consuming sozzled sticklebacks soon wore off – but only after they were rescued and propped up against rocks well above the high-water mark. To safeguard them while they sobered up, many volunteers kept a vigil from a discreet distance. Truly, an exemplary humanitarian effort, the result of which was that all terns were left un-stoned.

I can't make my mind up about birds in captivity. I guess that on principle I'm a moral objector, a peacenik rather than an animal rights activist. On the other hand, I eat chicken and I'm even partial to a bit of duck, so when I see farmyard fowl left free to roam over ranch-sized paddocks and splash about in muddy ponds, I don't feel so bad. That's a much better existence than being kept drugged in the dark and pumped full of feed. But enough about me. It seems as though the birds live happy, fulfilled lives right up until the moment their heads hit the block. They certainly look as happy as Larry; you can tell by their appearance. No longer worried about having to be at their best to find a mate, Khaki Campbells let their plumage go to hell. Geese turn into couch potatoes, sprout beer bellies and wallow in pee-green waterholes. Is lack of dignity the price of confinement, albeit in an open prison? I'm beginning to sound like a member of Anatidae International.

Such thoughts were put in a different perspective last autumn. I was out in the wilds of west Donegal where poultry use the roads and aged bachelor farmers, underpants drawn up over trouser tops like a badge of ancient rural culture, keep to the fields. Hereabouts is my ancestral home, a land where I don't feel embarrassed about my sputtery surname, which is everywhere: on buses, lorries, even pubs. I rejoice when a rustic psycho, mouth dribbling ribbons of saliva like a trail of spilled yoghurt, comes tearing around a bend on a tractor and nearly creams a whole herd of cattle. He's okay. He's a McGeehan. I won't break ranks with my relatives.

Well, I may have been birding in a region of Celtic twilight but what I saw was no illusion. A Muscovy Duck came hurtling out of a farmyard, legged it across the road and streaked past me like an Exocet on amphetamines. Muscovies are not normally the sort

The west of Ireland. A place where green-toothed endemics stalk the land (my next of kin).

Muscovy Duck – the only bird on the planet with a face that could stop a clock.

that you associate with rapidity, let alone being airborne into the bargain. As I watched, it banked and then collided with the bars of a gate. Hadn't it noticed the obstacle? It bounced back, recovered, and then sped off up a hillside. With a better view I understood why the thing was capable of such acceleration. It was not encumbered with the usual weight of a wart-coloured head. In fact, it had no head at all. I didn't see it after that, although further along the road none other than DIM Wallace vouchsafed that he saw something answering to the right description: "A Nessie-like bird moving at the speed of Lee Evans on a twitch."

Fortunately I don't know of any records committee with a jurisdiction over such a sighting, but there is an explanation. Nearby, a farmer's wife had been slaughtering chickens with an axe and, because her pet Muscovy was decrepit and almost blind, she decided to put it down. Gripped with a heavy heart she left it until last hoping that, after decapitating all the hens, she wouldn't be quite so aware of the big black one. Alas, nerves got the better of her and when she swung, she missed – and buried the axe in the chopping block. By the time she pulled the blade out it was hot, so that when the second stroke connected, it cauterized the wound. All of a sudden you had a duck with no brain up and running like blazes into the after-life.

Strange to think that, within a week, I should see some wild, non-kamikaze Muscovies along the Texas-Mexico border. That impending trip is one reason for me to leave this page. Another is because it is nearly noon and I recall a certain rule that applies to today's date.

June 1999
Birdwatch

One for the
road

When it comes to holding on to a good barber, I am like a human Mistle Thrush defending a supply of good haircuts to get me through winter. No matter how attractive the hairdresser, I have grown tired of making small talk and nodding gormlessly when the 'stylist' holds up a mirror to that part of the human body you never see – the back of your head – and asks if you like the result. Fair enough, I wouldn't want to walk around with a back-end Beckham bouffant but all that really matters is that, like a mandrill, I look okay from the front. Sod the rear view.

A few years ago I sat through a short, back and sides that warranted an entry in The Guinness Book of Records. It was the longest snip in history. By the end of it I needed Just For Men to restore colour lost during the length of time I'd sat under the scissors. Davy, who performed the Ten Weeks Younger operation, sculpted what little hair I had into a state of bonsai perfection. But he did something else that was just as impressive. He talked. He loves his work. Customers are his lifeblood. He is the sort of guy that makes you feel at ease and then, as if he was a friendly barman, you finish up telling him more than you tell your wife. Such as: "Can you do something about those eyebrows – I don't want to look like Dennis Healey."

He knows that I am keen on birds. However, I leave that baggage at the door. Well, not quite all of it. We swap stories. His are about hairdressing; mine are about birdwatchers. We have the human race in common. My first trim of 2009 was booked to be the last of his working week. Belfast's city centre streets outside his salon window were windswept yet full of life. "Unlike my hair, I hope." Tea was thrust into my hand while Davy turned to check a blonde under a hair-dryer and basted lacquer over tinfoil on a wannabe Brunette's head.

Lulled by the rhythmic beat of his roaming shears, I settled into a soporific state. Then he put me on the spot. "Well Anthony, any good yarns to tell me?" I didn't want to disappoint him. When cornered, I invoke a default strategy that never fails. I think of Mark Constantine. Mark is an army of mischievous thoughts moving across a landscape in search of an idea (for a laugh). "Believe it or not," I replied, "a friend of mine used to work in a salon too. But you don't want to do what he did." That was my way of adding a bit of introductory drama. It also stopped the scissors dead in their tracks. So I told him about the big red light linked to a klaxon and attached to the wall in Mark's salon. At a delicate moment during the application of henna dye onto hair roots - a time when the customer resembles someone

The author (right) in Belfast, February 2009. [Editorial note: Anthony was told to get a hair-cut for this mugshot and asked to leave plenty of background in the photograph for the inclusion of some 'atmosphere'.]

with a fresh cow-pat on their head - Mark would set off the klaxon and react with the shattering news that, as a part-time fireman, he had to go. In a flash, he did just that. Of course, only temporarily. You can imagine the horror of the bluff – and the warm afterglow of its full effect on both prankster and victim.

The effect was pretty immediate on Davy too. He reacted like someone exhibiting sudden pressure behind the eyeballs experienced after bolting a fizzy drink or ascending too recklessly from the ocean floor. I was glad he wasn't trimming close to an ear when I told him the punch line. That got the two of us going. Then there was the one about Mark bringing a dozen slide carousels to a talk and, picking the top one off the pile, proceeding to take an hour to project just 30 slides. As members of the audience grew increasingly worried at the sight of eleven more stacked carousels, he then finished the talk – but not before drinking in the sweaty looks of those trapped in front row seats. "What a bloke!" I sensed that Davy was on the verge of lionising Mark and perhaps dangerously close to emulating him. In fact, he already had. "The best laughs we ever had in this place," Davy said, "was when I rigged up a fake mouse to a piece of transparent fishing line and tugged it through the piles of cut hair lying on the floor around women's feet. That was – literally – a scream." "Superb!" I said, by way of congratulation.

Is it any wonder that today's haircut was progressing more slowly than a drifting continent? A final pass with the hairdryer drowned out any further attempt at conversation. But only temporarily. I said, "Would you like one for the road?" "Yeah!" he replied. Another voice butted in. "Hold on, hold on." It was the blonde. She was joined by the brunette and, as it turned out, everyone else within earshot. They had been earwigging our nattering and didn't want to miss the final instalment. All work ceased. Outside, people rushed past in the cold dark, pressing umbrellas into driving rain that glistened on the outside of the salon windows. Inside, big hairdressing chairs containing total strangers swung round to face me. Normally, when you tell a story to a few friends you can drop your voice as they all huddle round. Not this time. "Speak up," one matriarch snapped as she removed a towel from her head. Davy smiled as if to reassure me and then added, "no pressure."

The tale was a simple saga – funny at the time. Alas, maybe not any more. One of those 'you had to be there' incidents. The scene was blistering midday sun along the Rio Grande in Texas. Like local birdlife, Mark, Bruce, Ricard and I were hiding from the heat. Not so local children. They were diving from rocks. The river was very close – a cool python of water that promised instant relief from the furnace. I couldn't resist. Trees hung over the lazy current obscuring me from prying eyes. I dove in. Stark naked. Bliss! I shouted to the others to join me but the ninnies never budged. Then – nightmare – Murphy's Law kicked in. An American bird tour bus arrived. The leader decanted a bunch of mostly elderly female US citizens at the edge of the ford where we had parked. Apparently, this was a shoo-in spot for Muscovy Ducks and the middle of the day was a good time to watch one zoom past. I couldn't eavesdrop on this information since, at the time, I was watching Mark make off with my clothes. "Hey, who's that guy swimming in the river?" one of the female octogenarians asked. "Him?" Mark replied, "Well he used to be named Anthony McGeehan but now we call him Adam."

Even if the Three Stooges had wanted to save my blushes they were incapable of movement. They were out of control, holding on to each other, leaking air, unable to stand. Bruce seemed to make some attempt to assist. He steadied himself long enough to reach for his camera. There was nothing for it. I ran in full view of New Jersey Audubon's Texas 'Big Bend' tour. All I had for a fig leaf was a pair of binoculars that went some way to obscuring an outline which, one granny said later, reminded her of The Great Lakes. "I didn't know there was a Lake Inferior," Mark added.

The Belfast 'curl up and dye' listeners gasped and whinnied. They clearly enjoyed the story and – to them – its conclusion. I wondered if I should tell them the real finale? "Em, there's a postscript," I volunteered. I think that you have right to know the truth. I have never thought about making this a legal matter but, upon reflection, maybe it is time I did. I felt a weight lift. An inner strength filled my lungs and I bore witness. I waited for folk to wipe tears of laughter off their face. "A few years later," I began, this time trying to sound serious, "Mark invited me and my ever-loving wife to Bournemouth to attend his birthday party. I thought this was most gracious and, since we were strangers, he kindly promised to have a driver collect us at the airport. Mrs McGeehan got a new frock for the occasion but was understandably edgy about meeting a host of new people. As we strode into the arrivals hall I began to scan the various passenger names held aloft by cabbies. Before I spotted anything that approximated to even a bad spelling of 'McGeehan' disaster struck. My wife seemed to be felled by a thunderbolt. She wobbled, as though the shiny tile floor had turned into ice and she couldn't keep her balance. I grabbed her but she motioned me away. Throngs of holidaymakers turned to look at the commotion. "What's the matter?" I said. "It's you," she said. "Look!" I followed her gaze. At first I didn't recognize

the smiling face of the taxi-driver in front of me. Oddly, he seemed to know who I was. It appeared to be Mark's brother-in-law, Steve. Then he pointed up. Only then did I look up at the enormous placard he was holding aloft."

Davy said, "You mean, everybody in the arrivals hall could see it was you on the placard?" "Sure thing," I said. "Crikey!" he said. He continued, "Where is the photo now?" "All copies are utterly destroyed," I told him, "Mark has given me his word about that."

February 2009

Stuff
biodiversity

May. Now that the nights are longer there is nothing nicer than to plonk down in front of the computer and enter all the week's data for the bird reserve. Acres and pains. Oh I have so much to do. Avian flu to NFU; H&S and BAP, scarcely time for a BLT.

Volunteer: Very interesting. Bye-bye, here's my bus.

I thought that would do the trick. Right, if are any eco-warriors left, you can read the real tidings. Meltdown. That is the only word to describe recent events. All Redshank nests eaten, a score of Lapwing clutches AWOL, Ringed Plovers vamoosed and God-knows-how-many ducklings among the ranks of The Disappeared. The treasures of the reserve have been ransacked. All this after months of slog to prepare the habitat and fence out predators. The culprits are a pair of foxes and a 'gone bush' moggy. The real killers are the Red Peril. Recently I paid a visit to the grounds of a prison near Belfast. There, between 750 chavs and the rest of us, lies a grassy strip and a colony of Lapwings enclosed by the sort of defences that even a fox on a motorbike could not dent. Is this what I need?

Time to take a strategic view. After Guantanamo, Northern Ireland is probably the fence capital of the world. I hate them.

Every nature reserve has them. Sadly, they are needed. By protecting little parcels of land, people like me are the foot soldiers of conservation. We beaver away like a bunch of Jehovah's Witnesses, trying to keep our spirits high in the hope that one day the birds we look after will repopulate a Brave New World with no pollution or drainage schemes or monoculture crops. Years ago, when I was at university, there seemed to be more of us. We were scruffy creative types. Scruffy anyway. We were imbued with a need to help the planet. We thought that there might be a plan in which we could play a part. Government seemed to be waking up to its responsibility. I went almost wild with excitement when a whole tier of officialdom was declared 'The Department of the Environment'.

What was going to happen? Naively, I believed that politicians had turned visionary. I waited for news of some obvious measures. Declaration of 'Green Hearts' throughout the land: large zones where mankind was all but excluded and foxes could kill what they liked because the clock had been turned back a mere 2000 years to give Mother Nature a chance to balance out predators and prey in a healthy ecosystem. Remnant woods, humanized to despair by path networks, would be returned to wildwood. Moreover, although the bulk of the countryside remained under man's control, farmers would be paid to give a tithe to nature. Originally, they gave a tenth of the produce of land and livestock to the church. Why not now to God's other creations? New copses, meadows, ponds and arable acres of wildbird cover would enrich everyone's lives. And what about the townspeople? It would be illegal to cut down a tree without planting a replacement and every new building would, by law, require the addition of a natural home too: even in city centres where 'Swift bricks' could be incorporated in walls, or rooftops planted to provide habitat and reduce air-conditioning bills. Employment opportunities would spring up requiring a task force of environmentalists needed to stop nature going critical.

Wire fences are an alien concept to birds. Unlike us, they fly, solve problems of food supply by migrating and to avoid conflict have evolved complex signals. Who is better equipped to inherit the Earth? Is it even *close*?

What went wrong? It seems to me that a whole new generation has grown up unbrushed by the wings of natural history. Conservation has not become an ideological fountain pen. Did public attitudes change? Did the message not get through? Maybe I got the wrong end of the stick. Perhaps I should be looking for a new planet.

People are strange. We all have the same engine but react differently to influences. Years ago I thought that gamekeepers and wildfowlers were somehow bad people. How could they kill things? Now I have a certain affinity with them. We share affection for the natural world, especially the birds and animals. You think not? Read this – an account describing wildfowling on the (since reclaimed) mudflats of Belfast Lough in 1880: "Barrels, large enough to contain the shooter and his dog, were sunk in the ooze, until their top was about two inches above its surface, and were placed at up to one mile from the shore. To these the shooters resorted when the ebbing tide had left the banks sufficiently bare for their access at the flying time of the Wigeon – from dusk to dark. This flight over, the duck continue to feed where they alight and seldom fly within shot thereafter – except if the moon rises after the first flight. If the moon illuminates the banks the shooters remain in their barrels, constantly baling them out and cosseted with a water-spaniel who serves to keep the fowler's feet warm. But there are occasionally attractions connected with this shooting, incomparably superior to the sport itself. In a fine winter night, we behold the moon riding in majesty, the stars twinkling, the position of some beauteous planet marking unerringly the onward march of time."

Here is an interesting thought. If I had been around in 1890 and read those words I wonder if I would have followed in the fowler's footsteps? Instead my engine was ignited by a fresh set of heroes. As an impressionable youth, I was enthralled by natural history presented to TV audiences from Peter Scott to a monochrome David Attenborough. No jargon, no limit to the technical details of the subject. Passion flowed from their personalities and also the pens of others. I never felt patronised. I could see that they were completely absorbed by their subject and wanted to share it with me. That was enough to make me listen.

"The boy is keen on birds and nature study." I can hear my dad say those words when I stood in his shadow and he talked to one of his workmates. There was no stigma then. Now the reaction would probably be something like, "Ah-ha – a bit of a twitcher then?" Which shows how far the connection has drifted between birdwatching and cherishing the planet. The term 'twitcher'. On my housing estate it used to mean curtain-twitcher: a nosey-parker. Now the media have pigeonholed me as an anorak. I am supposed to be fair game for those who wish to poke fun at me for being eccentric. I feel repressed. I want to blame somebody for this branding, which ostracises me from the rest of society – the very people who should be wooed and won over to helping preserve Mother Nature.

Except it is not Mother Nature any more. It is biodiversity. Pass the brown paper bag please. I should have known that clever-dicks in the academic ecological ranks would throw a cordon sanitaire between the common people and attempts at conservation evangelism. Conservation is becoming sniffy. Acronym-speak is rife and even the very names of the things I love are reduced to lower case, turning an insult into nonsense (a unique combination). Pick the real species out of this mess: "All grey wagtails have yellow but only green-backed wagtails are yellow."

As I look at the birdy bits and bobs scattered from hell to breakfast around this PC, I cannot help thinking that they resemble a kind of pyre upon which I have built a life. Is there an optimistic note that can be dredged from all the detritus? I will try. Yes, it would help enormously if birdwatching could somehow reinvent itself and become a mainstream popular science once again. Or that we might find a leader who would inject some turbo-charged thinking into bringing nature and humanity together again in a benign way.

Could it be that we need an –ism? Think about the forces that control the modern world. Capitalism, socialism, communism (to name just a few). We are a gap. The environmental movement needs a makeover. Long or silly names are doing us no good at all. 'Environmentalist' with its 16 letters is hard to say after two pints; 'Green' is just plain soppy and the party's choice of colour could yet derail peace in Ulster. 'Conservism' is the way to go. If our mantra is to conserve then our party activists are Conservists. So much the better if confusion reigns and we steal voters from David Cameron. But there is another thing. The policies will be coined 'Conservitarian'. This is important, for herein could lie salvation. Human nature being what it is, party splits will be inevitable. It should not take too long before the zealots break away, line up behind a charismatic extremist and call themselves Free Conservitarians. Come the revolution, everywhere will be closed on Sunday and alcohol will be banned. The resultant reduction in the emission of greenhouse gases might halt climate change and unharvested oats, hops and barley could feed thousands of declining seed-eating farmland birds. Wanted: one ayatollah with birding experience.

November 2008

Caution!
Humans ahead

Saint Patrick is credited with banishing snakes from Ireland. What he did for reptiles Sharon, the reserve's cleaning lady, is doing for spiders. She hates them. I don't get to see the carnage but I read campaign reports about it in note form. Sharon works two nights a week, yet the two of us haven't actually met since the last millennium. We communicate by yellow post-its, which keep everything from toilet crises to Christmas greetings down to size. The onset of spring and the season's plant growth ushered in the following exchange of communiqués.

"Anthony, the Big Daddy of all spiders is holed up in the jungle growing again at the front door. Please leave pruners. Sharon."
"Sharon, that's my favourite honeysuckle. Please don't prune it as severely as you did last year. Anthony."
"Anthony, what honeysuckle? Sharon."
"Sharon, that's what I mean. Anthony."
Keeping Sharon's hands off the natural world can be a problem. But not always. Take foxes, that prowl the place at night.
"Anthony, there is a fox mess in the car-park. My employment contract covers only humans. I'll leave the wildlife to you. Sharon."

Now that the evenings are bright she recently met her first birders who visit the area after work. Her first impressions were incisive and possibly revolutionary.
"Anthony, a bloke with a face resembling a melted candle and dressed like an unmade bed demanded to be let into the main observation room. I told him it was closed for cleaning. He said he was a twitcher and a friend of yours but I called the police anyway. If this is what birdwatchers are like then I think Darwin should have looked for the missing link right here in Belfast instead of wasting his time in the Galapagos. Sharon."

I like Sharon. She is a housewife by day and cleans to pay off debt. In her job she can afford to be as blunt as a French lorry-driver. Sometimes I wonder what she would make of mine. Maybe I flatter myself that people might think I can help with basic bird identification. Such as when a woman fumbles through *Birds of Europe* trying to put a name to the female Reed Bunting perched just a few metres away. I ask, 'Would you like to know what bird that is?' She replies, "Oh, it's all right. I've found it on page 498. It's only a Rock Sparrow." Now what? There was a time when I would have gently explained that her misidentification was a plausible and understandable slip.

The visitor said, "Let's look this one up in the book: brick-red chest, patterned back and some yellow on the beak. It's a Red-throated Pipit." "Madam," I replied, "you have the makings of a talent."

"What's this?" the woman in tweeds exclaimed. "it has the body of a Pheasant and the face of a head mistress."

However, this approach can go down like a lead balloon when indignant novices feel patronized and stick to their guns. These days I tend to smile sweetly and say, "You may well be right."

Women ask most questions. "Excuse me, is that a kind of duck?" "Yes madam, that is a female Teal." "And what about this one?" "Actually, that is a female Teal too." "Okay, I think I've got the hang of Teal. So what about the different one over there with the bright green on its wing?" At this finale of an ignominious hat trick it is best to sugar the pill. "The bad news is that it is another female Teal. The good news is that you are in good company because Saint Peter also denied Jesus three times and for God to create bright colours on the wings of female waterfowl and confuse beginners is both unchristian and downright silly."

Men, on the other hand, prefer to suffer in silence. For example, a sleeping Pectoral Sandpiper could be tucked away among dozens of snoozing Dunlins and a bloke who desperately wants to see it will clam up and not enquire about its whereabouts. Is manly reticence genetic? A midwife once commented that male babies take longer to deliver than female babies. Could this bear out the theory that, even at birth, men are reluctant to ask directions? Exceptions occur, chiefly when machismo is at stake. A dreaded situation can develop when a family group inadvertently mingles with a line of telescope-peering gullists. If someone watches gulls for more than 20 minutes without moving, I hold a mirror under their nose to check if they are still breathing or can be pronounced clinically dead. With a jolt, a figure in the silent row of anglepoise lamp look-alikes exclaims "Ring-billed Gull!" and I am left to field questions from an audience of puzzled onlookers. The husband asks, "Why the excitement?" I tell him that the species has flown here from North America. His curiosity is aroused. Not only does he now wish to see the star bird but he also wants to show it to his kids, one of whom is sucking a dummy.

The alleged Ring-billed Gull is half-buried in a great swarm of Common Gulls and can scarcely be distinguished by the narrow white fringes to its tertials. Fear not. I begin the painstaking process of directing the parent and unruly offspring to the quarry. First I orientate the dad. I say, 'Can you see the tall block of flats in the distance?' He can. Good man. Next I fan his ego and let him line up the gull on the shoreline with the flats behind. Has he got it – the really big one with the jet-black back, pink legs and bit of a red 'ring' on a yellow beak? He has. Congratulations and smiles all around.

'It's been a pleasure listening to you.' I seem to say this a lot. The biggest bores deliver monologues that last longer than most marriages. One insufferable gargoyle is impossible to avoid. To be cornered by him all you have to do is have a pair of binoculars draped around your neck. Now you are in for it. The ritual begins when he innocently borrows your binoculars for a casual perusal. Dismissively, he compares them unfavourably with his own, and then proceeds to quote from an encyclopaedic knowledge of optics. The android will know everything from what the letters B/GAT stand for on Zeiss, to how to spell 'Swarovski'.

There was a time when I concerned myself with weighty issues such as whether green armoured Leicas resolved a sharper image than black armoured Leicas. I have since discovered that the capacity of every human brain is limited. So I have deleted all files containing optical data. It is wise to do this on a regular basis. When you get right down to it, there are only three things worth remembering – your wedding anniversary, the date of your wife's birthday and, in the event of one of those being forgotten, your blood group.

June 2002
Dutch Birding

In darkest
Belfast

Apart from a terminal avocation as a birder, what is your day job? Mine is a diplomat. Add to that labourer, window-cleaner, reed-cutter and general dogsbody and you've got a pretty comprehensive picture of what a nature reserve warden has to do. I work in the middle of Belfast docklands or, to be more precise, on the adjoining reclaimed waste-ground that developers cannot be bothered to fight over any more. This land, for the sake of 'conservation', has been set aside and trumpeted as an innovative urban reserve – a new concept in introducing the public to the natural world. Indeed.

Except that the place is something of a poisoned chalice. It's a pig's ear and I'm expected to turn it into a silk purse. I wouldn't have taken the job but for the fact that this is my native city and I stood by powerless for twenty years while most of the area's habitats were systematically ruined, only to see the remnants spared in the nick of time. I'm not complaining. Few people are given something to work with that is already in good shape – look at what Sven Göran Eriksson has inherited. The irony in my situation is that I'm the classic poacher turned gamekeeper; the arch trespasser of the 1980s has become the upright custodian of the 21st century. And, would you believe it, not only do I liaise with the port police and military authorities – former

adversaries – but I've discovered that they are also pleased that things are finally happening to protect the birds.

It's uplifting when the people from whom you least expect to earn respect, show signs of giving you that very thing. But can you really trust them? I know all eyes are on me and that every conservation advance will be scrutinized, chewed over and discussed out of my hearing. If things go well, fine. However, make one slip and all credibility will disappear faster than a dot com company. So a game of cat and mouse is being played. I am the mouse but the cat can be a bit gullible. Recently the cat took the form of Sergeant McDonagh, a man apparently with better eyesight than mine. With advancing years I can put up with impending baldness but the prospect of fading eyesight is no laughing matter.

It transpired that, from his imperious sentry box overlooking the roadside along which three of us were planting a hawthorn hedge, Sergeant McDonagh had noticed numbers of birds and other animals that I had missed, thereby exposing my fading eyesight, if not growing incompetence as a birder. Here are three examples. (1) Instead of an estimated 20 rabbits attacking our hawthorn seedlings after dark he'd seen 'hundreds'. (2) The number of Golden Plovers roosting on nearby grassland did not total 850 but amounted to 'at least a million'. (3) I was wrong about the identity of the white owl that hunted in the general vicinity. Based on his description of size 'wingspan bigger than a Landrover', it couldn't possibly be a Barn Owl and must be either a Snowy Owl (first record in County Down since 1843) or a creature that special agents Mulder and Scully should be told about.

This, of course, was incredible news. Think about the implications. An esteemed member of the security forces whose exaggerations would be believed – even in a court of law. I was presented with a diplomatic coup par excellence. Here was an opportunity to infiltrate the docklands' mass media through

an impeccable source. The last thing I was going to do was to query any of his census figures or meticulous attributions of wingspan size. Quite the reverse. I dropped a few statistics that he might find interesting. Did he know how many thousands of trees we intended to plant and what a great help a mechanical digger would be? That took care of immediate needs. The rodent problem took a little longer to crack but, in the end, he managed to beat my claimed personal best of shooting 20 rabbits in one night which, evidently, had the added benefit of frightening away all the scores of others.

God bless Sergeant McDonagh, his heart is in the right place. Sharon, on the other hand, is not on the same wavelength and

Sunset at Belfast docklands.

Black-tailed Godwits have a sinister side that, quite frankly, some people find scary.

regards working for birds in an entirely different light. It would be unfair to describe her as Cinderella. She is the cleaner who has taken over my nocturnal round of maintenance duties in the reserve's posh visitor centre, grandly referred to as the Observation Room. It really is lovely and provides amazingly close views of, among others, Teal, Wigeon and Black-tailed Godwits.

I felt sorry for Sharon who, because she arrives in the dark, doesn't get to see the spectacle. I suggested that she should call during daylight. "Would that be overtime?" I said it wouldn't, I just thought she might be interested. "Listen big fella, I'll leave the birds to you and your patience; I'm only paid to scrub down the Institution Room." Sharon has a certain directness and an imperfect way with words that I can relate to, or thought I could. Her early attempts at washing the tiled floors were disastrous. No doubt she was keen to impress and to do a good job, but she was using too much detergent. When she goes home at night the floors are wet and look okay but the dried out versions that greet me in the morning resemble a skating rink. Reluctantly, I phoned her. She said, "But I do all my hospital floors the same." The awful truth dawned on me. Her calling the building the 'Institution Room' was no accident. She assumed I ran a clinic or some kind of asylum. Even her remark, "You and your patience," took on a new chilling connotation – obviously, the true transcription was "You and your *patients*." My God, she reckons birdwatchers are nutters!

Although our backgrounds were far from similar, I thought we shared at least one thing in common: a desire for high standards in cleanliness. I was mistaken. On warm evenings millipedes are attracted to the lights around the entrance door. Their presence sickens and disgusts Sharon. She vacuums them up. When I

commented that they were harmless and could stay, she was appalled. "If I had vermin like that climbing up the walls of my house I'd move out and get the public health people in." This statement implied that if I tolerated such insanitary conditions at work then I probably lived in abject squalor. I felt like I badly needed the services of a Max Clifford. I desperately wanted to claw back some street cred with Sharon who, by this stage, was doubtless drawing parallels between the reserve and either *One flew over the cuckoo's nest* or *The Adams family*. Comparisons with the latter were reinforced when I got an urgent communication from her supervisor. Sharon, the fax said, didn't want to come to work anymore because the premises were "haunted". What?

The supervisor told me that she'd heard, "blood-curdling noises" outside the building and found a handwritten note addressed to me by one of the volunteer staff confirming "goblin" activity. She read a photocopy of it back to me. When she got to the line "250 of them are almost pecking at the windows", the penny dropped. I said, "Oh, *those* goblins. I think you'll find that they're not winged evil spirits but simply birds called godwits." We were both relieved; we both laughed. Somehow I don't think Sharon saw the funny side of the incident. In its wake I'm trying hard to remain on friendly terms with her, which requires me to pay even closer attention to any other misgivings that she might have. Sharon may not like birds but I don't want her to become afraid of them. There is too much at stake. Let's put it another way. If that damn Barn Owl happens to pick the wrong moment to fly past the Observation Room's windows I could be back on toilet duties for the foreseeable future.

April 2001
Dutch Birding

Time to
take him away

Wanted: care home with sea views **by Mrs McGeehan**

Anthony does not have the brains to be sneaky. He is a one-trick pony who thinks that I don't know his secret dodge. And what is it? It is this. When he is supposed to have hoovered the house – but hasn't – he sprinkles some Shake n' Vac about the place and leaves the vacuum cleaner sitting out in the open – still connected to the plug. He thinks I am fooled. Feigning housework is one thing but suppressing news of a rare bird is, if you believe all the manly moralizing, a hanging offence. Has he done that? Well, yes he has. Furthermore, the rarity – a Pallas's Warbler – was a first record for Northern Ireland. He dipped on it, nobody else got to see it, so he kept his mouth shut. Even worse, the guy who found it, a novice birder, got none of the credit.

I know the incident has always rankled with him, a skeleton in his cupboard. It occurred just after we were married and, at the time, he was certain the technique he used to try and see the bird would catch on. He felt that he had chanced upon a hidden truth. He told me, "Do you know what Winston Churchill said? Most people stumble into the truth but pick themselves up and walk on regardless." I asked him what on Earth that was supposed to mean. He said that there are hidden meanings, which, if you don't discover their meaning, mean that you will never know

the meaning of certain things. I told him to quit sounding like Dan Quayle. He tried again. "Put another way, it is when someone uncovers a startling fact or innovation but is greeted with scepticism and branded a pseudo-scientist. Eventually they are proved right and the discovery becomes mainstream." You mean like the guy who discovered the microwave oven – he was derided for a time? He said that wasn't a good example – too domestic. However, compared to my analogy, what I heard next was scary. In a nutshell, he was suggesting that today's psychics would become – you will like this – tomorrow's physicists.

I don't know the names of many rare birds but Pallas's Warbler will always stick in my throat. I'm sure they are pretty. Anthony used terms like 'gem' and 'jewel' when he first described what one looked like. That was back in the days when I was just getting to know him and I had asked him to tell me the name of his favourite bird. Then I enquired about where I came in his estimation. I aimed far too high. I should have picked a low-ranking species and rephrased the question: "Darling, given a choice between Magpie and me, which would you choose?" His reply made me sound like a piece of Ratner's bling. So I had mixed feelings when he arrived home from work one October and told me that he had news of Ulster's first Pallas's Warbler and instead of what we had planned, he would be off to see it at dawn.

His mate Billy Chambers had detected it. "Billy Chambers?" I said, "Since when did that freak becomes a birdwatcher – all he does is drift about scaring people while water divining." "That's how he discovered it – with his crystal." I said, "Oh, this better be good." I started laughing. I said that I didn't realise I had married a fourth dimensional husband. I said, "You shouldn't listen to that man or to weird music." "What weird music?" "You know, that stuff you were playing the other night." "But that was Simon and Garfunkel." "I know," I said, "but what about the line 'Hello darkness, my old friend?'"

Bit by bit, I got him to spit out what was happening. East winds blowing all the way from Siberia at Halloween (you couldn't make this stuff up!) had dumped dozens of Pallas's Warblers all along the east coast of Britain and as far west as the Isle of Man.

Hah! So he can set a candlelit table after all.

He was certain that several had reached Ireland. Alas, if nobody knew where to look, they would never be found. So far, so good. Up to this point he seemed to be remaining steadfast to his Earthly beliefs. By chance – soon to be cited as fate – he bumps into Chambers. This screwball makes money by dowsing. He wanders across farmland 'hunting the pluck' with a hazel fork that jerks when it passes over groundwater. Supposedly he also has the ability (moments after dangling a crystal over a personal effect and putting on a serious face reminiscent of a rattlesnake with toothache) to see where you have left your car-keys. After rumours of one lucky strike, people who had lost not only bunches of keys but their husbands and wives were asking him to find loved ones in different postal districts or even faraway zip codes.

Apparently, as often happens, the whole thing started after an innocent remark. When Chambers – who is at least mildly interested in birds, although only as Gothic icons – heard that Anthony suspected that there must be a Pallas's Warbler on this side of the Irish Sea, he offered to help. The pair of them pored over an illustration of the species in Lars Jonsson's *Birds of Europe*, and Chambers got out a brass pendulum. He took a 'reading' off the plate and then, slowly and carefully, gyrated the pendulum over a map of Northern Ireland by dangling it from a piece of string held between thumb and forefinger. He did not move his body or speak. Anthony watched in silence, entranced. The string moved quickly, a spinning wick against the knuckle of his yellow finger. Then there was a downward convulsion. "I've got one," he said. Where? It was on the Copeland Islands, lying off the east coast of Northern Ireland and within sight of the Isle of Man – the perfect spot. Sadly, Anthony greeted the breakthrough with bitter disappointment. While the method was convincing, he could not get out to the islands to check or, as he put it, "to see the bird." "Would you like me to try for another?" Chambers said. Not knowing the most likely areas to search, he drew expected blanks across inland counties. At one point he strayed close to the border with the Irish Republic. Anthony swiftly corrected him: "Don't look there, I want the Pallas's for Ulster." Then, just when Chambers was running out of land, he found another. It was on the southeast extremity of the Down coast; about a 90-minute drive away. Alas, there simply wasn't enough time to twitch it that day. Besides, more accurate directions would be needed.

"Get me a map at a large enough scale and I will pinpoint the twig if you like," Billy Chambers proclaimed. Anthony dashed out and bought the Mourne Country Outdoor Pursuits Map, scale 1:25,000. Chambers switched to his favourite crystal, "This machine finds eyes in needles," he hummed. Within seconds of unfolding the map, the telltale oscillation was back. The target was in the grounds of a large estate. Having filled me in with the main details, Anthony's voice dropped and slowed to a crawl. Was he beginning to question his sanity? Just a tiny bit. Certainly, he realised that he faced a dilemma. Could he claim all the credit if he saw the bird? Should he suppress Chambers' role in the matter? Should he put the news out on Birds of Ireland News Service? No, better to do this single-handed; the implications of twitching through the use of a medium were too mind-boggling to contemplate.

That night he made a flurry of phone calls to Chambers. Right up to the time that he left the house at 0700hrs, the two of them were in contact. He was in top form as he went out the door. Why? Chambers had been checking the map through the night and confirmed that the bird was still there at 0655hrs. When Anthony got to the spot he felt that he had entered the spirit world. The habitat was perfect, truly heavenly. The site comprised a stream outflow from a pond surrounded by willows and alders. Small birds were everywhere; the air was full of high-pitched sounds. And there, feeding busily in 'x-marks-the-spot' was a small, warbler-sized bird with every one of the hallmarks of Pallas's Warbler – double wing-bars, yellow rump, the lot. Except it wasn't a Siberian fairy light. It was a Siskin.

I thought that he would be changed after that, shaken out of his world of blissful self-deception. Not really. An 'unresolved' conclusion was arrived at. Since Chambers was not a birder he had actually been right! What? He had found a bird matching the correct description. How was he to know the difference between two tiny green-white-and-yellow birds? The mistake was failing to rip out all the look-alike plates from *Birds of Europe* before dowsing started. According to the chief sorcerer, 'interference' had resulted from not isolating the unique appearance of the intended subject. So, close, but no cigar? My husband, now exuding a saturnine sense of scientific rigour, stressed that, for a real test, the bird in question would have to be unmistakeable without any risk of confusion. I said, "Would an Ostrich with its head in sand be appropriate?" He tut-tutted. However, I couldn't argue with the thrust of his reply, which had at least some logic behind it. In October 2007, with high winds from America, he said that he was going to repeat the experiment but this time by choosing a wacky American rarity with a tail like a Pheasant and a face like a Budgerigar. He said, "After the storms at Halloween, I bet there'll be a Mourning Dove lurking somewhere in the west of Ireland."

December 1995
Birdwatch

Gyr
crazy

Jack London's *Call of the Wild* did the trick. Reading it, I felt the icy breath of an Arctic winter on my neck. The book gave me a word tapestry of snow and darkness, huskies and men, wolves and caribou. The elements of harsh adventure were described but not the birds that went with them. Similar frustration is experienced watching Polar Bear documentaries when the cameraman pans past an Ivory Gull feeding on a seal carcass and cuts to a five-minute close-up of mother bear fondling baby bear.

Slowly and excruciatingly, Bruce Mactavish – my friend who 'endures' winter birding in Newfoundland – started to fill gaps in the ornithological narrative. He knows where to stick the knife. Where I had fantasies he had memories. He categorizes every one of the 177 Gyrs that he has seen. As the detail poured out, I began to feel like his therapist. He lives in a grey world – the colour Gyr. With mounting trepidation, I asked what constituted Code Ten, his scale's climax? "That is when you don't just hear the sound of an approaching Gyr – you feel it. Wind turbulence from a big low-flying female causes involuntary human head-ducking. If she is a white-phase *candicans* then a supreme man-meets-Gyr moment is consummated. The pleasure is deep. There is no greater high."

The trouble with Gyrs is that they are not predictable – a quality that also makes each encounter unforgettable. No, they do not hide and yes, coming in every shade of ghost, they ought to be as conspicuous as a Basking Shark in an aquarium. However, supersize dining – Ptarmigan al dente is a popular dish – means a lot of time is spent chewing the cud. Moreover, plotting the next meal may involve hours of sussing from a watch-point on a frosty promontory whose countless lifeless boulders easily disguise the ultimate winged life form.

Today's inhabitants call it 'The Rock'. Newfoundland was first noticed by Leif Eriksson and other Vikings around 1000 AD who founded a settlement along its barren north coast before pushing south to Nova Scotia where the land was so much better that they named it Vinland (after local wild vines). Leif converted to Christianity and was well offside before immigrant waves of Irish, Scots and Welsh arrived. The island sits on the cusp of an iceberg-dotted Arctic sea and the warming waters of the Gulf Stream. The currents collide but the result is the worst of both – cold and wet – which gives rise to a local acronym RDF (rain, drizzle, fog). People get lost in that stuff, sometimes for centuries. Bruce is one example. He is the Viking who wandered off birding and missed the longboat south.

This was a moment that I would gladly have prolonged into a week. I cannot find the words to describe it, but I was in heart attack country and survived.

I envied his home turf. When the fog lifts a land of endless toothpick trees and calm humorous people is revealed. Newfoundlanders live in quiet wooden houses painted pastel and enjoy the best sea views on Earth. Roads are a driving thrill – no cars and single highways leading to small communities twinkling in the darkness like distant galaxies. On fall mornings Bruce dines on wild berries, a breakfast he sometimes shares with juvenile Long-tailed Skuas feeding in front of him on blueberry barrens.

As the last flocks of White-rumped Sandpipers caught cool October tailwinds and fled south, and the sombre russets of autumn disappeared under November snowfall, I felt a growing sense of unease. One day soon Bruce would march outdoors and there it would be – the first Gyr of winter. A triumphant bird hanging in the wind perfectly lit against a sky of Sinatra blue. Its watcher would throw back his head and yell for two solid minutes. Then he would email me. I couldn't take it any more. Item one on my letter to Santa was a winter trip to Newfoundland. I caught a daytime flight in January and sat glued to a window as the plane came into land. I was already on Gyr alert. The snowy winter prairie of Canadian airports is a favourite haunt of Snowy Owls and you-know-what.

"Guaranteed." That was the word he used to describe my chances of communing with *Falco rusticolus*. Mactavish may not have had a shoo-in lined up but he did have a plan. We would spend ten days in the field – mainly looking up. The species list would be low on variety, stellar in quality. He was right. Downtown in St John's there were Pine Grosbeaks in gardens and Bald Eagles over parking malls. Stranger still was the fact that my Gyr leader, a noble savage armed with binoculars, took me shopping. He had warned against bringing gaudy outdoor gear from poncy ski boutiques back in the UK. In an army surplus store he specified a camouflaged grey jacket lined with goose down. He checked for deep pockets. "Buy it," he ordered, "you will smell like prey and the pockets are big enough for a bottle of Screech rum – you will need that to keep warm."

At the end of Day One it was clear that neither beginner's luck, the luck of the Irish, nor the miraculous medal that my mother had sown into my binocular strap, were doing any good. Still, I was living the dream. It was a renaissance of constant surprises. The itch up my nose was due to air freezing the forest of fuzz inside my nostrils; because I had to shake off snow and ice

from boots and clothing, it took even longer to undress to go indoors than it did to get ready for the outdoors; when I asked for a kitchen roll to dry thawing-out hands and was given a slice of bread instead, it was because the local phrase for kitchen roll was 'paper towel'.

It was a fabulous trip. The air sparkled like Kodachrome. Headlands appearing a lunar distance away were reached in minutes, not hours. Scanning lonely turquoise bays peppered with Little Auks attracted attention from chatty locals who spoke with burry Dublin accents and invited you in for tea. I translated for Bruce who, coming from Ottawa, had struggled to understand the natives for years. Days passed as I waited for a sign – maybe a flinch from Mactavish when a tiny white dot registered on his gimlet retina. It was about time to quit and go home happy but Gyr-less when, on the last evening, I saw the silhouette clawing the air above a cliff. Below lay Quidi-vidi Lake, a major gull roost and happy hunting ground. The shape cast a spell. It rode the updraft as if treading water. It was looking and searching – surveying the menu. My throat went dry. When I swallowed to speak, my Adam's apple became stuck. I could not get the three-letter word out. Lightning flashed in my veins. The sun had set behind the bird's frigid escarpment, its final rays tinting snow and sky pink. I had to look close to make out detail. Soundlessly the speck hung in my universe. Then it flipped and rolled and turned into a big black Goth. It was a Raven. I had, in Bruce's words, fallen for the 'Rum and Raven Trick'. "Never mind," he said, "Your birthday is in February and I still have my winter sick leave to take. Here – take another swig."

April 1994
Birdwatch

Bitter and twisted

Have you ever noticed how unthinkable it is for a birder to write as much as a line on a postcard without attempting to grip off the recipient of the missive? Friends and acquaintances who, throughout the year, display nothing but the most prosaic of qualities when it comes to putting words on paper are suddenly transformed into screenwriters of Spielberg proportions when they reach foreign soil. But what do these gasbags produce? Having been on the receiving end of a regular stream of unsolicited letters, cards and faxes, I can tell you that, as far as I can see, their interest in the natural world is wafer thin. They hit the ground running and disappear with the cheapest hire car available in hot pursuit of an armload of lifers. Once their desire is sated, the blarney starts to flow homewards. Responsible, God-fearing family men and women like you and I become the hapless victims of these poison pen birding hooligans. It is about time some were named and shamed. This month's words are not my own. So, for once, I don't have to worry about propriety or expletives in this column.

Quito, Ecuador

Ola! Got a lifer before we even got off the plane: Fidel Castro. He was here for some kind of knees-up with the country's new socialist president. The place was bristling with moustaches wearing suits and soldiers dressed like Sergeant Pepper's Lonely Hearts Club Band. Security was tighter than your wallet but we were waved through unchallenged. Why? Probably because I was wearing that ratty Che Guevara tee-shirt!

To begin with we didn't pay any attention to all the fuss – for one thing we clocked an ANDEAN CONDOR over a mountainside – but then we learnt that it was impossible to rent a vehicle, even a motorbike. The reason was that every sissy Yank in the capital had cleared off with a hire car. Apparently, they whiffed revolution in the air and panicked when they heard that Fidel's mate won the election. Good start, eh? We've been stuck here for five days now and if we don't get a car soon we'll have to sleep outdoors as the hotels are really expensive, despite being dives. To crown everything, both 'Gringo' O'Grady and I have gone down with altitude sickness. I suspect flying straight into a city 12,000 feet above sea level might have something to do with it.

Yesterday, Gringo developed toothache that nearly sent him off his rocker. We found a dentist called Gonzales who said he could fill the tooth. I'd like to tell you that he did a 'speedy' job (ha-ha) but it was actually a bit of a disaster. The drill broke in Gringo's mouth and he screamed. At this Señor Gonzales attacked Gringo (maybe he thought we were going to sue for malpractice) and I had to take sides in the matter. If we don't get out of this city soon we'll be broke or in jail, but we took a taxi to some super habitat and scored more new birds in a morning than you will see in a (light) year. Crested Guan was sensational – a bit like a big hairy Chough – and we managed to get through to the Irish Birdline with a forged credit card. Sounds like there isn't a sniff of a good bird at your end. Glad you are seeing bugger all. We feel MUCH BETTER NOW.

Cape Spear, Newfoundland

Ant man, I thought I'd send you this pre-supper fax to let you know what birding was like this January morning. We got a foot of snow last night so I only made it to the seawatch spot by following a snowplough. The sea ice was just a quarter mile offshore, which pushed the auks and eiders in real close. Saw nine King Eiders flying among about 1,000 Commons. I tried to ignore the many Thick-billed Murres but as you fantasize about this species so much, I forced myself to look at them. Still can't understand why you get excited about such a boring bird. You must be sick in more than a physical way. You would have loved my looks at one. It landed among the drifting floes and got trapped.

This happens quite a lot. Thick-billed Murres are so fat and stupid they have problems getting airborne from confined spaces. The good news is that I wasn't the only witness to its plight. A white Gyr spotted it too. It powered over the ice, grabbed the Thick-billed and plucked it in full view for 20 minutes. Incredible

Bruce Mactavish prepares to french-kiss a Thick-billed Murre. Birding friends will go to a great deal of trouble to make you feel bad.

Vancouver, British Columbia

Dear Dipper, good morning from a ringside seat at the world's greatest bird feeder. I'm sitting here beside a big log fire, mug of coffee in hand, with all kinds of birds just inches from the window. I'm glad I came over for Ted's wedding now. The other day I picked out a really gorgeous thrush and looked it up in the book. Varied Thrush! Apparently, this is one you haven't seen before: a blocker no less. I have several photos of it. I'll show you them when you pick me up at the airport next week. Don't be late. I hope you and your lovely wife are okay and that the kids are behaving themselves. Mother.

December 1997
Birdwatch

'Now don't take it the wrong way but this one was just like you - it ate the leftovers that the dog wouldn't touch.'

sight. A pity the Gyr's pristine white chest got messed up with some Thick-billed guts – kind of spoilt the nobility of the GREAT WHITE HUNTER. I'm sure you'll agree. I'll send you a snap. Did I forget to mention that I had the camera? Today I could've used a telephoto lens that focused closer than 20 feet. ☺ Well, must dash. Supper has arrived. I'm having 'turr' tonight. Remember what that is? If it's good enough for a Gyr, it's good enough for me. I'll save you the wishbone. Cordially, Mactavish.

Luck
of the draw

Before it was turned into a marina for the nautically insane, Bangor's harbour was something of a Mecca for winter rarities. Nothing too rare – a wintering Glaucous Gull, maybe a Little Auk or the brief stardom of a Mediterranean Gull. That was enough to make a walk along the town's old wooden pier a regular fixture in the winter birding calendar.

Then, when a local fisherman reported a tame white gull (with black spots) that spent a Sunday afternoon promenading around his bait, opinions were divided on the bird's true identity. An oiled Kittiwake? A leucistic, albinistic or arthritic something or other? Even a Feral Pigeon might provide the answer. Furthermore, he said it walked like one.

It couldn't really be an Ivory Gull, not when several birders had checked the harbour, including Big Umbrella who had been there for a stroll with his fiancé that evening. Well, she must have hypnotized him with her magnetic looks for the big dork clearly didn't look below eye level. Otherwise he would have found the real love of his life.

Next day news of the fisherman's sensational discovery reached the mass media. The town's Mayor was interviewed on TV and asked to explain how the bird had arrived. That wasn't the question local birders wanted answered. What they couldn't understand was why they all missed it and how the bird that was destined to make Bangor famous had been found under their noses by a non-birder.

Bingo players experience a similar phenomenon. Take my mother, a regular combatant who pays her dues, puts in two nights a week but never wins top prizes. She wouldn't mind if one of her mates cornered the big money, but they don't either. A visiting relative, doting aunt or first-time player ("So how do you win? Oh yes - just cross out all the numbers. Silly me!") are the sorts of infuriating tyros who scoop the loot. Rank amateurs to a tee. Even worse, I know my mum feels that it is somehow *her* money they take, *her* luck they usurp. So much for novenas to Saint Anthony, patron saint of lost causes. Although, technically, that constitutes cheating. Sorry mum.

In birding, the roulette wheel is capable of spinning even worse luck. Take the case of the immigrant English birder flogging a new local patch in Ulster that included a tern colony. The birds were mainly Arctic Terns, but there were also Common Terns and occasional Sandwich, Roseate and Little. When a 'for sale' sign appeared on a bungalow overlooking the area, a hastily clinched property deal brought them all within telescope range of a lounge window. With exclusive regular watching guaranteed, his chances of discovering a rare tern were sky-high. Or so he thought.

Days later an out-of-town birder arrived on the bungalow doorstep, breathless, car door flung open and engine running. He obviously wasn't on a social call. "Black and White-winged Black Terns at the colony." Ouch! A double whammy, but surely the resident birder deserved to find them?

Is it easier to tolerate the luck of non-birders noticing unusual birds that prove to be rarities than to accept the good fortune of a fellow birder? At such times you can sympathize with the situation that the prodigal son's brother found himself in. If he'd been a birder he would have been the hard-working, dedicated type who is out winter and summer in fair weather and foul. Then along comes someone with the Midas touch who reaps a disproportionate reward, such as finding a Siberian Rubythroat in his own back garden. When that happens you feel like complaining to a higher authority. "But Father, you promised to give me the Ring(-billed)." Such patent injustice, but what can be done about it?

The moral of the story is this. Life, and birding, is a lottery. No one has a monopoly on luck. The only predictable thing about rare birds is that they are unpredictable, which is why they are rare. So enjoy them while you can, be generous with your praise for the jamminess of others and look forward to sharing in it – which you will, eventually.

Both birders were delighted to see the rare terns at the colony and – perhaps by way of fitting compensation – an even bigger rarity showed up a year later. A Forster's Tern. Pay dirt at last and a thoroughly deserved reward for the prescient investment in bricks and mortar and daily telescope vigils. Not really. The Forster's was, ahem, my luck of the draw. Sickening, isn't it?

March 1993
Birdwatch

Is God anti-twitcher? Then how come he bestows the honour of finding dream-birds on non-birders?

Med Gull
madness

'FAO Mr Bruce Mactavish, St John's, Newfoundland, Canada.'

Believe me, I could have done without that tale of your recent Ivory Gull encounter. Also, deepest sympathies on seeing only four Gyrs this winter. How was your Easter Sunday birding? Early morning was absolutely useless here. Briggs Rocks quiet, Strangford the same. In the afternoon I decided to dodge an impending visit from the out-laws and nipped back to the Briggs 'just for a quick look', you know the usual palaver. The tide would be dropping and the wind had picked up from the east, so gulls ought to be gathering at the outfall and scoffing the best of the holiday pickings. To be on the safe side, I brought the camera.

The action was okay and pretty soon I found a stunner. A Med with a full sooty hood, 'big banana' white eye crescents and a driller so bright red I could pick it out from the Black-headed Gulls on bill colour alone. Amazingly enough, this babe was a second-summer, as it had black wing markings. It settled on the water and, after yet more luscious looks, I swung the scope back through the throng. I had probably just said to myself, "If I don't find another Med in this lot I should order myself a white stick," when – BINGO! – there was a first-summer. A real chameleon age. At rest they look like a Black-headed with a hangover (smudged black eyes, heavy head, bloodshot bill), yet in flight you have to be careful not to throw one away as a Common Gull. In a melee like this the snow-white under-wings and crisp black secondary bar do the trick for flight ID.

So, holy jumping jelly beans, what to do now? Although it was pretty crazy even to think about, I decided to strip from the waist and walk the 100 yards to the outfall. I guess you won't be too surprised at this because, as birders, it is the kind of act that we are put on this Earth to contemplate committing. The first hurdle was a seaweed-covered concrete wall that contained the sewer. Beyond that was a series of rock outcrops with deep channels in between. Unseen beneath the surface the rocks were either sharp-edged or encrusted with limpets and barnacles. Because it was Easter Day it felt appropriate to walk barefoot.

I suppose compared to the Labrador Current the Irish Sea is definitely warmer. It was probably just a little above freezing point. On the plus side, this helped anaesthetize my feet against the lacerations I sustained en route to the last rock. I had to be quick as the wash from a passing tanker was due

Mediterranean Gull, first-winter. An acquired taste. But, like Guinness, once you like it you are addicted.

make sure I wasn't in heaven, although the smell might have been a give-away.

Now for the bad news. In less than three minutes, I shot all 36 frames. However, I had the presence of mind to bring an extra roll. JUST FOR YOU, YOU WEASEL. I had secreted it in a private place, but not where you think. My gonads were glacier-cool in the seawater, so I had to stick the film up my armpit under a rolled-up shirtsleeve. Now the Meds seemed to be in a mood to party: full passes, formation flying, synchronized dip-feeding. What a species. God must have been on the sauce the day he made that bird. Why else would he have stuck a big red snozzle on a tar-black head and finished it off with the wings of a dove? Definitely Gull of the Universe.

Then, just as I feared, I heard the whoosh of the approaching wake and felt the surge as a wall of water hit my knees. The thought of not bringing this exclusive report to you stung me into a hasty retreat that a Rockhopper Penguin would have been proud of. So here I am and there you are: Med-less, unfulfilled, leading a life yet to be lit by the lustre of Med Gull under-wings (first-winters) or upper-wings (adults).

I arrived home – late – to a house full of complaining relatives who were quickly silenced and backed off when I told them what I had just paddled through. I'll leave the last word to one of the heirs who seemed to please the crowd when he said, "Dad, how are we going to get you off this birdwatching stuff?" Maybe one day he'll understand the experience and savour its deeper meaning.

to hit any minute. All these things kept my mind busy and purged of thoughts of the liquefied turds that I had just waded through. For fear of drop-offs I hoisted the camera high above my head, which was just as well, as the bins got drenched by a brown wave crest and were now useless. It didn't matter. Naked eye, I saw the second-summer. I panned with the camera and peppered it with an opening salvo of about ten frames. As it banked and began its run back through the pack, I couldn't believe what I was seeing. It passed three more immatures before dip-feeding beside a Little Gull! I had to slap myself to

June 1996
Birdwatch

Franklin's
hangover

"You can go if you promise to redecorate the hallway and stairs." My blood sugar levels were shot to hell yesterday – Sunday 17 August 1997 – so I agreed. I'd just come in from a morning's birding. To save time, I had eliminated breakfast from the schedule. Arriving home punctually half-an-hour late at 12.30, I found the house deserted and headed straight for food – a banana and a packet of crisps. Five minutes later I still hadn't eaten a thing and was back in the car hurtling towards a hastily organized rendezvous, my knees doing the steering while both hands stuffed much needed carbohydrate down my throat.

The reason for the panic was the wife's scrawled news flash. Eight words did the damage: "Eric rang. Franklin's Gull all morning at Clogherhead." The impact of that communiqué was made all the more powerful by an earlier incident. Friday 7 May 1993. About to board a plane to New York, I stupidly phoned birdline from Heathrow. Guess what? A Franklin's Gull, the most talked-about absentee from Ireland's most wanted list, had turned up. Flying west over the Emerald Isle that afternoon, my two birding companions, an unsympathetic Englishman and a garlic-breathing foreigner, had to restrain me from hijacking the plane. Our destination in America, New Jersey, contained a small backwoods town called Franklin. Here, I was forced to eat

breakfast next morning. It got worse. Over coffee, the pair of them tried to reach out for some form of personal support – but only to break their fall as they slid under the diner table in jibbering ecstasy when an Aretha Franklin track came on the radio.

When I got home two weeks later the bird was long gone. Waiting in the hall was an advance proof of *Irish Birding News* that contained the understated, self-effacing description of the finder's (Peter McDermott's) emotions: "I had found the long-awaited Franklin's Gull and it was time to relax, but not before retiring behind a sand dune to do a little dance of delight, give a few whoops and indulge in some air punching." Thanks Peter, I became suicidal after that – but not before I corrected a couple of typos and fell on my sword by polishing up the text. I resisted the urge to be a killjoy and add the usual wet blanket line, "This report is yet to be accepted by the national rarities committee."

So now, four years later, the long vigil for a second Franklin's was over. But would I see it? Before I could get the latest news, the phone rang. It was my brother. He sounded like a CNN reporter, "Where the hell have you been all morning?" I replied, "Watering the lawn and feeding the roses, where do you think?" "All right, all right. I guessed you were out birding. Have you heard the news?" I told him I had.

He said, "Hunter-killer has just arrived to pick me up and we're about to leave to collect Einstein McKee. Hunter says there is room for you, although he has the trots after a rough vindaloo last night and you'll have to sit behind the driver's seat." I said, "Tell him not to light a fag in the car. I'm on my way, see you in 20 minutes."

I'd like to tell you that, in the heat of the day, we swept soundlessly along country roads in air-conditioned comfort to a quarry that greeted us with fantastic looks as it hawked insects over grassy fields before settling right in front of us on a sun-kissed beach, its plumage flushed pink by the glow of a triumphant sunset. In reality, our 70-mile journey was plagued by roadworks, diversions and Sunday drivers who travelled so slowly that their back bumpers were a death trap for speeding wasps and bluebottles. A drive that should have been completed in less than 90 minutes took over two hours – which undoubtedly cost us the bird. It flew off going high and inland shortly before we arrived. The species was becoming a Frankenstein.

As the day wore on and we wandered further and further afield checking endless flocks of gulls, our chances and our patience started to wear thin. That's not to say we hadn't found some birds which, under less stressful circumstances, would have been pleasant surprises: such as three Mediterranean Gulls and a bunch of Roseate Terns. In a weak moment – probably a flashback to his years studying for the priesthood, a calling finally relinquished because of the unsocial Sunday working hours conflicting with birding time – one of the party commented: "Oh well, it's been a good day really. The juvenile Med Gull was worth the trip." We snapped at him. Such heretical sentiments were premature, plus they might blight our luck. Hunter said, "Don't be a Jonah, weren't you taught anything about the power of superstition?"

It was about time to quit so we split up in a last-ditch attempt to cover more ground. Inland, the sun was beginning to set in a prairie scene that must have beckoned the Franklin's ever westward. Darkness was settling and you had to look hard to sort through the gulls flying onto the coast. So when Hunter's car came roaring down the road with its headlights blazing, I wasn't suspicious initially. When I noticed he was alone, the thought occurred that perhaps the bird had been discovered and he'd come to fetch me but then I remembered the vindaloo residue and realised why the others preferred to remain out in the fresh air for as long as possible. However, when he screeched to a halt and yelled, "The drinks are on me!" I knew that four Franklinless years were about to end. He'd found it all right, squeezed among a pack of roosting Black-headed Gulls, its grey morning suit upper-parts, black hood and massive white eye crescents making concealment impossible.

That was when the celebrations started. We, the kind of people who are irresponsible enough to drop everything for the sake of dashing off to enjoy a rare bird, may have a number of failings, but temperance isn't one of them. The full effect of last night's revelry will take a while to wear off. When it does, I imagine the warm satisfaction of the overall event will last considerably longer. I intend to carry that thought with me for a time, especially when I go out to buy some paint and wallpaper later today.

March 1997
Birdwatch

Franklin's Gulls behaving themselves on a North American bible belt lake, unaware of the two-fisted, night-long drinking caused by one of the species. Truly, that prodigal gull received a real Irish welcome.

The luck of the **French**

Let me see, can I remember the day I saw my first Ross's Gull? That is a ridiculous question. I can instantly recall not only the moment but also the agony of the sleepless night when the news broke and, to boot, the many Ross's-less years wondering if I would ever clap eyes on such a mythical creature – for me the equivalent of Antony's Cleopatra. The species was first claimed for Ireland as far back as 1842 when William Macgillivray included it in his *Manual of British Birds*, volume two, page 254, with the remark: "This species has once occurred in Ireland." For a while the record pre-dated the first for Big Brother Britain (one shot in Yorkshire in 1846 or 1847) until it emerged that the Irish individual didn't actually exist. What happened to it? No jiggery-pokery was involved; the explanation was much more mundane. William Macgillivray's printer was the culprit since he had inadvertently changed one letter and metamorphosed Iceland into Ireland.

Close, but no cigar. From then until January 1981, Irish birders felt that some kind of hex had been put upon the species. We had not found any, whereas British records stood at a dizzy 20 by this time. All that came to an end when a teenager named Guy Hamilton discovered an adult dip-feeding in a coastal harbour late on a snowy New Year's Day. That night almost no one was at home to be told the news over the telephone so instead people got hastily scribbled notes shoved through their letterboxes proclaiming: 'Ross's Gull at Portavogie – be there at dawn', which stunned them into sobriety.

What is so special about a diminutive pink gull from the Arctic? At the risk of sounding heretical, I don't think Ross's is quite the most beautiful gull in the world – actually, I prefer Mediterranean Gull – but the species wins hands-down thanks to its aura of rarity and tale of discovery. There is always a good story when someone's name is commemorated in a species' title, which keeps the connection between past and present alive. History is reborn when you see the faces of men such as Pallas, Eversmann, Blyth and Hume. It's strange to gaze at our dead ancestors. They are presented like characters out of Dickens. Pallas has a white wig, wears a tunic and has medals pinned to his chest. He looks like an ornithological George Washington. All of them are old and, if they were alive today, could easily find work as stand-ins for Father Christmas. I'm not keen on that kind of image. It is better to let your mind drift away and see them in their prime – young pioneers doing the kind of things that we wish we could do. Take James Clark Ross.

Born in London in 1800, James went to sea at the age of 12. He was sent on naval duty to the North Sea and the Baltic but he wasn't left to fend for himself. His uncle John was on the same ship and the pair were close enough in age to strike up an almost brotherly friendship. Probably, they were thick as thieves. For the next six years they were inseparable and in 1814-15 they surveyed the coast of the White Sea off Archangel. Then in 1818, with John as captain of the whaler *Isabella*, they went in search of the North-west Passage. Their orders were to round the north-eastern point of America and sail on to the Bering Sea and Kamchatka. There, the ship's journal was to be handed over to the Russian Governor who was to send it overland to London to communicate their success. Sadly, they could not find a navigable route through Canada's Arctic islands and returned home defeated. Worse, John was castigated by sections of the Admiralty establishment for not trying hard enough. James made further attempts to find a way in 1819-20 and again in 1821-23. Hold it right there. Can you imagine young blokes today doing this sort of stuff? Remember, James had gone off twice to search for the North-west Passage before his twentieth birthday. Clearly, he was not a quitter.

So, where does Ross's Gull fit into the story? We have only sketchy details to go on but, never one to let a dearth of information stand in the way of a good yarn, I have embellished a full account for posterity. Close to midsummer's day in June 1823, James was with a shooting party near Alagnak on Canada's Melville Peninsula at 69:15 N. During the previous week, 230 ducks had been shot to provision the ship's stores, mainly King Eiders and Long-tailed Ducks streaming north to reach thawing breeding grounds. James had a reputation as a marksman and, single-handedly, he must have spotted the approaching gull as something different. It was flying near a flock of Arctic Terns, that it somewhat resembled, save for a white head. Being small and providing little eating, such quarry would not usually have been procured. But not this time.

"When the Ross's Gulls follow the trawler, it's because they think sardines will be thrown into the sea." E Cantona.

You can imagine what happened next. The sharp-eyed adventurer singles out the pink and white bird with the grey thundercloud underwings and longish, jaeger-like tail. There is the slap of a hand on a wooden gunstock, the click of the trigger and then the crack of the musket going off with a mighty blast,

the bullet ripping through the icy Arctic air. With no more sound than that of a falling angel, the bird flutters down to Earth and lies dead on the snow. From that first moment its looks have captivated. Even the expedition log waxed lyrical about the gull's endearing appearance, enthusing about the 'beautiful tint of most delicate rose-colour on its breast.'

I narrated this saga to a friend of mine recently. It passed the time on a night drive to Galway on the west coast of Ireland where we hoped to see the living legend. These days, the species is a virtually annual rarity but my pal had never seen one before. So I concluded the account by emphasizing the chances of dipping out. "Ross's Gulls," I informed him, "are notoriously erratic and some people seem destined never to see one." Of course, I believed this to be nonsense. It was simply my way of cranking up the tension, because the Galway bird had been around every day for a month. But not that day. Remarkably for Ireland, the grim news was relayed to us in broken English by four glum-faced French birders. They had come all this way but had to leave at noon. I was surprised that they had not seen a Ross's Gull on their native soil until they told me a harrowing story that sounded like an episode from the *X Files*. "As a nation we are cursed," they said, "since no living French birder has seen a Ross's Gull in France. It feels like we are the victims of a malaise, bewitchment or evil incantation. By 2000, 86 Ross's Gulls have been seen in Britain – mais nul pointes pour nous. Pourquoi?"

You could feel the hurt, insult and sense of sadness. Gallic pride in ruins. I tried to cheer them up by pretending that the bread-guzzling Ring-billed Gull at our feet was a fitting

substitute. I nearly got the guillotine for that slander. Being a Sunday morning there was the possibility that the bird had gone to Mass. Maybe this explained its absence? Sure enough, just as the crowds spilled out of the nearby Catholic church, the Ross's materialized to the chimes of the Angelus, like a true Holy Spirit. The French greeted its appearance as only the French can. They whooped and cheered and left on a roll. "Phew, that was a close shave," my friend said. "Closer than you think," I replied. "I didn't tell you that James' beloved uncle John Ross served with distinction in the Napoleonic Wars, was wounded fourteen times and spent a miserable time as a prisoner-of-war in no less than three squalid French jails. Apparently, after that, he really had it in for Les Bleus and is reputed to have invoked some long-standing fee-faw-fum against them."

Postscript: Empirical evidence suggests that, indeed, John Ross's malfeasant embargo held firm until its spell-by date expired at the end of the last millennium. Since then, Ross's Gulls have started to appear on 'that side' of the English Channel.

April 2002
Dutch Birding

A trip to
Iceland

By whose skilled hand was Lapwing made,
A-glow with colour of every shade.
Wings of lapis lazuli,
Ink obsidian for an eye.
For sure the artist has to be,
No less than Salvador Dali.

Lapwing is my die-in-a-ditch species. I enjoy every one, even though I see some almost every day. From grannies to generals, this is a bird guaranteed to impress. I tell teachers that Crayola never put such iridescent colours in crayons for fear children would colour outside the lines. Consequently, I find it really unfair that a bird that gives so much gets so little. What do I mean? I am referring to the blighted hopes and foiled productivity of many breeding attempts. You have to take your hat off to the species for embarking on a nesting strategy delightful to behold yet exasperating for the birds. If Trappist monks were Lapwings they would have regular screaming fits.

The annual treadmill of disappointment starts in March. The first clutches of speckled eggs are laid at the end of the month. The female sits right out in the open for four weeks and prays.

Where I work, most first clutches fail. During the day, all available Lapwings scramble to assist in defence of a nest in peril. They are fearless. I have seen birds dive and hurl themselves against Buzzards and Marsh Harriers to ward off danger. At night it is different. They cannot deter foxes. Replacement clutches are underway by late April and since most of these go the way of the first, a third and final attempt is made in May. Some victories are snatched from – literally – the jaws of defeat. It is a huge relief to see a tiny crack in the first egg. Within a day, all four chicks will be led away to begin a month of furtive feeding and hiding. Although the parents do all they can to shield wayward fluffy babies from Magpies, whole new generations can be snuffed out within hours of being born. It is hell out there – not that those bleeding-heart liberals who defend Magpies and foxes would know anything about it.

There was no dithering when Mark Constantine bowled me the perfect ball. He delivered Magnus Robb, a purebred sound recordist. All my eulogising about Lapwings would finally have an outlet – if Magnus and I could combine displaying birds and perfect recording conditions. Neither was going to be easy. First, the birds. Our best opportunity would be in March when pairs were on breeding territory but before nesting started. Naturally I wanted the Full Monty of wheezy wolf whistles, intakes of breath, and high, rasping crescendos that accompany the daredevil flips and rolls of the birds' crazy Biggles-in-a-biplane aeronautics. But there was something else - the wing noise. I said, "Magnus, our best chances will be at night. If we get calm conditions the birds will go mental and in the dark they might be calling while passing low overhead. I have sat directly below a tumbling Lapwing and the effect is hair-raising. You hear the approaching whump of creaky sinews that precedes a banshee wail. One sound begets the other. In stereo, that would be really something."

The second worry was the recording conditions. In a gesture reminiscent of Doctor Strangelove, Magnus waved his hand over a map of eastern Northern Ireland and said, "Well, you can forget that lot." At a stroke, the counties of Antrim and Down had been nuked – as far as the chances of finding silence were concerned. What about Lapwing breeding islands in deepest Fermanagh? Weren't they uninhabited? "Even if no one lives there, there could be generators running through the night, transatlantic flights overhead, or flocks of bleating sheep – remember March is lambing season."

To begin with, our endeavour was dogged by day after day of wind and rain. To make matters worse, if the weather improved, I still had no idea where we should go to find Lapwings and stillness. Before that, two other targets occupied our time. Song Thrush fills the void unsung by other birds at dusk. A shrinking violet by nature, the species comes alive when it opens its bill to sing. Maybe it likes its name. One soggy day ended with two treetop Pavarotis indulging in a bout of lung-wrestling while

Magnus cowered and tried to deflect thudding raindrops from hitting his microphones.

The other target was Dipper. This was my wannabe ace-in-the-hole. I had located a nest on a ledge inside a long, 50-metre tunnel beneath a quiet road. Apart from the tinkling of running water, there could be only one other sound – the singing Dipper. I built a hide and floated it downstream. I didn't mind the hassle of steering the Thor Heyerdal construction over rapids and past entangling briars and rhododendron suckers of Conan Doyle vintage. I knew the Dipper's favourite song post, and it dutifully obliged with daily chants just inches from the hide's canvas covering right up until Magnus arrived. Heavy rain swelled the burn and the bird's perch was submerged. It still sang, but from somewhere else. Furthermore, a gurgling stream was now a river in spate. It sounded like Niagara Falls.

I left Magnus to persevere. The hide was cosy and dry. He brought a head torch and read for hours. That gave me some thinking time. Pick an island, any island, as long as it has Lapwings, Skylarks and Rock Pipits. What about Inishbofin, west of Galway? Too risky. They are building an airstrip and the sound of rock-hammers might spoil the chances of natural acoustics. What about Aranmore, west of Donegal – all the targets bred there? No way, I did not want Magnus to see a beautiful place defaced with the thoughtlessness – wrecked cars and gratuitous squalor – that blights most Irish islands. A favourable meteorological prediction of high pressure over the Saint Patrick's Day public holiday drove me to Google. I spent a morning checking weather charts and boat sailings. I had the makings of a plan. A two-word text from Magnus ("Dipper sang!") signalled that maybe, at last, our jinx had ended.

"So, Magnus, let's not do complicated. Perhaps listeners might prefer to hear just the relaxing sound of running water rather than the silly chirping from a Dipper? Oops, what have I said!"

When I told him where we were going – Tory Island, off north Donegal - Magnus, who has survived a week-long force majeure miles from nowhere on Siberian tundra, rockfalls along the Euphrates, and dizzy nocturnal descents on Macaronesian seabird cliffs, looked worried. I assured him that the place lacked carnivorous fauna and bloodthirsty brigands and – less welcome news – sultry womanhood. He articulated his thoughts with soulful Scots gravitas, "Anthony, my big concern is the racket that 200 Irish citizens might make during Saint Patrick's Day on an island just three miles long and half a mile wide." I told him not to worry. "No one will be outdoors, let alone working, or straying more than a toilet's throw from a pint."

Rather than fretting about the recording conditions, we had a more pressing difficulty: I didn't know if the ferry was running. For some reason, Monday sailings had been left blank on the island's web site. Maybe it was the skipper's day off? Surely Saint Patrick's Day would be different? I tried contact numbers but none was answered. I phoned my mother who originally hailed from Donegal and asked her to try some relatives who still lived there. She phoned me back. Good news and bad. There was definitely a boat at nine o'clock in the morning but nobody knew whether it was leaving from Magheraroarty or Bunbeg. The two piers were ten miles apart. However, we could get breakfast at my aunt Mary's but could I collect some faulty flat-pack furniture at uncle Eugene's and bring it back to Belfast for a refund? I lied and said I would be travelling by motorcycle.

Magheraroarty was ship-less so we drove to Bunbeg. It was the same. However, locals informed us that the skipper would collect all passengers at nine o'clock and drive us to where the boat was moored. And so he did. We were the only travellers. As we rounded a corner the boat swung into view. In total calm and glorious morning sunshine, it was the epitome of a painted ship upon a painted ocean. At that point a car shot past us going like a blue streak in the opposite direction. "Whoa!" the skipper exclaimed, "Hold on tight, that was Brigid. Jesus, Mary and Joseph. I'll have to turn." We spun around and Magnus whispered in my ear, "What the hell is happening? I only saw one person in that car. Is this how Lourdes started?" I explained that there was a full stop between Brigid and Jesus. "Around here," I said, "Jesus, Mary and Joseph is a polite way of saying 'Oh shit!'" We caught Brigid at Bunbeg. Like us, she too had neglected to check her tealeaves that morning to ascertain the boat's departure point.

Seen from the sea, the coast hereabouts is undeniably beautiful. Its capes, promontories and mountainous hinterland are arranged like so many sharks teeth that bite the incoming white horses. Except there weren't any white horses. It was the finest Saint Patrick's Day in living memory, the boatman said. By the time we reached Tory we had seen 20 Great Northern Divers and the same number of perfect reflections. Although a minor detail, we had no idea where we might stay. Nowhere opened until Easter but that was about a month away. However, there was talk of a hostel and the woman who ran it lived on the island.

We got directions to the place and I rapped the tiny door, which was open. Nobody seemed to be home, yet the kettle was boiling. Where was Snow White? There was a gratis communal cupboard with tins of food, jam, boxes of cereal, packets of soup, and tea and coffee. Leftovers from previous guests. Things were looking good. We might not even have to go to the shop (a possibility which appealed to Magnus' sense of Scottish frugality). Alas, there was no fresh milk. Piles of tourist literature were neatly arranged on a wide table. Books on Irish castles, lighthouses and islands, brochures on independent hostels, train and bus timetables, and a copy of *Gaelic for Dummies*. Another volume looked strangely incongruous. It was the *Rough Guide to Iceland*. Magnus asked, "Why is that here?" I replied, "Can't you work it out? Some fool has blundered. Mistaking that second letter was where the purchaser went wrong." Then the woman arrived, milk in hand.

Before I had time to ask if the place was officially open for business, she was in full flood. "Make yourself at home. Would you like a cup of tea? I'll make up the beds. You can stay as long as you like. But you can't stay in the gable dormitory. Two Germans take that one and I know they are not here at the moment but they said they plan to come over at Easter. Are you here for the birds or is it diving? You wouldn't get me in the water. Nobody can swim on this island. They say that if you are going to drown it is better to go quickly rather than exhaust yourself swimming first. Do you like football? Tory is Man United mad. Isn't that Ronaldo some fella? Those Brazilians are unbelievable – or is he Portuguese? Mind the front step when you come in from the pub. If the door key sticks, jiggle it in the lock. The salt air is the death of locks around here. That's why nobody locks their doors. I'm sorry to dash off but old Mrs Gallagher is being buried today. Poor woman, she was an insomniac, you know. The doctor said she died in her sleep but how could that be? I always said that man was a quack. God bless, now!" With that, she was off, although clearly not out of words. Before English replaced Gaelic as the lingua franca in Ireland it is claimed that

in parts of Donegal people had such vast vocabularies that they never used the same word twice.

Outdoors, the world was miraculous. It was as though every bird on the island had awoken from a winter of hibernation and was in a mood to party. We had a symphony on our hands. Larks strummed the sky and pipits parachuted to the ground in spiralling song flights. Great chasms at the high eastern end of the island formed fantastic natural echo chambers for the lisping trills of Rock Pipits.

The afternoon became a lullaby. Displaying Redshanks, Ringed Plovers, Oystercatchers and Snipe were all around, their calls set to the tune of the North Atlantic at rest. What about Lapwings? Although plentiful, they were quiet. We knew why. They were pacing themselves. So were we. If the weather held, they would start to rock in the dark. Although it felt like sacrilege, we declared a siesta. I watched the evening news while Magnus checked leads and charged up batteries. Everything seemed to be in good working order – I didn't hear a single 'Jesus, Mary and Joseph'. We ventured out just before dusk. Although we didn't know exactly what to do, we did have a plan. Put simply, we were going to walk slowly across the entire island and periodically sit quiet in the hope that we might find ourselves at the epicentre of tumbling Lapwings.

Proper darkness came on with breathless stillness just before midnight. A dusk breeze fell away and the Lapwings seemed to sense the calm. All across Tory, they responded to the signal. Overhead, the moon was almost full, the beam from the island's lighthouse swept the ground like a giant metronome, and there was a silver sheen of moonlight off the sea. It was bright enough to see your shadow. Hunkered down behind turf banks and following the sound of a displaying Lapwing, it was sometimes possible to catch an ET glimpse of a winnowing Peewit against the moon. The western sky was chequered with high clouds but only stars hung over the few houses that still had lights on. It was cold but we didn't notice. Several times I was sure that the microphones must have caught the Doppler effect of approaching wingbeats, followed by point-blank calls as their owner swept past. I was dying to ask but I knew that we had to be patient. It was a magical night and I felt greatly reverenced by the show that Mother Nature had laid on. Except when the moon shone on our upturned faces, we must have looked like dozing sheep – a part of the landscape, ignored by the birds. Eventually, and with that sense of trepidation that goes with opening presents on Christmas morning, Magnus made a comprehensive check of his efforts. I thought I could detect smiles in the dark. Then, sure enough, a thumb was cocked. He'd caught the banshee beat!

We hit warm beds at 0500hrs but I could not sleep. I was still wired. When I did fall asleep I had a nightmare. In it, I found myself stuck in a cheesy moment. A pushy radio host doorstepped me with the question, "You are a birdwatcher – can you tell listeners what is so special about the song of a Skylark?"

Struggling to describe something that is not reducible to words and conscious that I might debase the very bird itself, I replied, "I love the sound. It reaches deep inside and pulls at my soul. I am transported back to childhood, lost in the daisies, aware of larks overhead although taking more notice of the disquieting buzz of nearby insects. In those days I heard the song but didn't listen to it – there is a difference. I used to lie on my back and through cupped hands try and spot the singer, a speck against the blue. I watched its quivering wings riding the air, face to heaven, broadcasting for all it was worth, like a radio operator tapping endless Morse code. Nonchalantly and without warning, the music stops. I yearned to find its nest. That was why I paid so much attention to the song: I wanted it to finish so I could search – in vain – for an egg-filled lair beneath a tussock. Hence the song is lost on the young. You have to be over 21 to comprehend. The convulsion of liquid notes is an elixir that enables you to relive the nostalgia of youth. I imagine it stored all winter, a kind of audible fossil fuel that bursts into life on the first sunny day each spring. A Little Brown Job it ain't."

Just as I am coming close to sounding dangerously sublime, the interviewer butts in and announces a commercial break. Dog food is advertised, followed by a jingle for baby wipes, and then the weather report. Before that she had said, "Don't go away folks – we will be right back with Anthony's little feathered friend." Damn journalists. Why do they belittle the finer things in life? I woke up in fit of sweat and rage. Despite being wide awake, I felt like reminding her of what Shelley said in *To a Skylark*:

Teach me half the gladness
That thy brain must know;
Such harmonious madness
From my lips would flow,
The world should listen then
As I am listening now.

March 2008

Skylarks are the essence of Mr Happy.

Gulls n' **roses**

Mrs McGeehan *gives some tit for tat*

I'm lying here realizing that action is going to be slow on a Saturday night in a hotel room in the west of Ireland. It's our second night but he still hasn't unwrapped the complementary bottle of champagne that was part of the deal. He is snuggled under the sheets right now but only to check his digital shots in conditions of total blackout. Apparently, he needs to be in the dark to see exposure details. He said, "Think of a bride's dress photographed in sunlight – all the frilly gunk would be burnt out. Gull plumage is the same, so I have to be careful that I don't lose delicate details." It wouldn't take Dr Anthony Clare to see where his real interests lie. To make matters worse, the digital age has undermined his machismo by removing one of his two main roles in our marriage – that of putting film in my camera. That just leaves reaching for those high spots that I cannot reach. Namely, the upper branches of the Christmas tree where his long arms are handy for hanging the fairy lights. Until he finishes looking at his snaps in austere silence, I am the invisible woman. I'm not allowed to speak and he certainly won't be talking to me. Maybe I'll go out for a drive in the car. At least the woman's voice that narrates the Sat Nav will talk to me.

We are right on the seafront and the traffic from bars and restaurants sounds like the Chinese army on Mayday. I suppose

I'm having a pretty good time, despite the underlying motives. It began when I dropped a hint that I would like a Saint Valentine's surprise. Amazingly, he went all out and booked a hotel. In Galway. Beside the docks. Gulls from the bedroom window. Still, the city centre is nearby and reminds me of Edinburgh's Royal Mile – and there are plenty of shoe shops. I amused myself watching couples sipping lattes in the afternoon sunshine while he lay among bread-guzzling gulls on the slipways, not noticing what he was lying on. I kept a safe distance, observing one of my little rules: Put Down Your Husband, You Do Not Know Where He Has Been. He was in danger of becoming a tourist attraction in his own right. I said, "Where's your hat?" He looked up from the ground and said it was in the car, that he wasn't cold – or did I mean that a hat might protect him from a direct hit from overhead gulls? I replied, "Neither. I was thinking that some of the curious passers-by might make a charitable donation if your cap was beside you."

I wished that I had walked on. I was press-ganged into chucking bread into the air so he could try for flight shots of swooping gulls. Except that I couldn't do it. "Like this," he said, hurling lumps high in the sky. I said, "Anthony, don't you know anything about women? We're no good at overarm throws."

He said, "If I look and smell like a dead seal the Iceland Gulls might come close."

Well, it turned out that the chief object of his desire was so sated that it wouldn't rise off the water anyway. The star was an Iceland Gull. Purely because of its pretty name I took a look at it. Blokes wouldn't understand that. More people would warm to birds if they like the names, especially when a person is in the title, such as Eleonora's Falcon, Jack Snipe or Sooty Tern. "What about Lady Amherst's Pheasant?" "Wrong feel," I said, "that's *Tweed* perfume, Marks & Sparks, and a queen mother type with a creepy feather in her hat." I reminded him about our honeymoon. "What was that lifer you nearly dipped on? I'll never forget it. You were away for two hours in 30 degrees heat and had deliberately taken the car keys so I couldn't turn on the air conditioning – a stupid waste of fuel, you said – and I saw a pink bird popping in and out of a nest right outside the driver's door. "You mean Common Rosefinch, although it was called Scarlet Rosefinch back then." I was aghast. "Who did that to its lovely name?" The long answer was some need for clarification; the short answer was men. Is it any wonder birds are declining?

At first I thought it was the male menopause. Sweaty nights, mood swings and staying up into the wee small hours. I discovered the explanation when I was leafing through a magazine. My stars had been clipped out. He had wanted the article on the reverse side of the page. I began to notice similar surgery in newspapers. I said, "What's with all the current affairs lobotomy? Are you introducing Sharia Law in this house?" It turned out that he was working on a book. I said, "About what?" His answer was cryptic. "Well, I suppose it's about birds, although they are only the tip of the iceberg." I told him that if he mentioned a single word about our marriage he would be in even bigger trouble than the Titanic.

His first problem was trying to merge ancient history with the modern day. In other words, he had to throw away his quill and learn to write using a computer. I would be shaken awake at 0300hrs to be informed that there was a crisis. The PC had frozen. Could I do something? He said, "The stupid thing quit and it keeps flashing the message, 'To restart, turn monitor zero n', what the hell does that mean?" I said, "Can't you understand English? Press the big green button; it is saying 'turn monitor ON'." Switching to a nocturnal existence has taught him other things. He didn't know we had a milkman. Because the author was AWOL, I found out that our bed had a middle third that he has occupied illegally for years. I get up in the morning to find that every light has been left on. A work colleague commented that ours is the only house in Ireland visible at night on Google Earth. Into the bargain, he never locks doors. I challenged him about that. He said, "I didn't know we lived in a dodgy area." I told him that it wasn't the television I was worried about – it was his precious optics. "Remember," I said, "I lost everything in the Post-Natal Depression." I reminded him about the 'big lens incident'. I had been vacuuming and the Hoover lead caught his camera and – unknown to me – knocked it onto the floor, dislodging the lens. He discovered it in two pieces next morning. He said, "Don't move a thing, I'm going to call the police." I said, "But I did it. It was an accident. I'm your wife, for heaven's sake." His response: "This is no time for nepotism."

His mother warned me about him. She went into labour late on a Wednesday and he was born next day. 'Wednesday's child is full of woe; Thursday's child has far to go.' That accounts for his dreaminess, a slippery slope for a man of his age. For example, he has started to hum the same tune over and over: 'My Way', of course. At this rate he will soon be doddery enough to read

"Darling, this really is for the best. Trust me."

'How to be a Bad Birdwatcher'. On the other hand he always says, "Go ahead, enjoy yourself, don't worry about me," as though he has some good fairy buzzing around his shoulders. But I do worry. Sometimes I don't understand what makes him tick. I was there with him on Inishbofin last November. He bumped into that Mourning Dove just as it was getting dark. All he saw was a silhouette doing a runner at dusk. He said that what should have been the best moment in his life had been ruined. He was on autopilot when he spoke those words, so I forgave him. I could see that he was upset. Tormented. He leaned against a stone wall, forlorn. What was he going to do? What could he do? I was anticipating a fingertip search for DNA-yielding poop to prove the bird's identity, but no. I said, "Why are you waiting? All the birds have gone to bed." He replied, "Oh, I don't know. I guess all there is left now is the religious aspect of birdwatching." Please, can somebody tell me what that is supposed to mean? Fortunately the dove was alive and kicking next morning. He got the bird and I, for the meantime, got my husband back. Goodnight.

February 2008

Heaven
can wait

Sometimes an incident in life results in a dilemma that refuses to go away. What can you do? People say, "Talk about it – communication is the best form of therapy." Personally, I think people could be dead wrong, but I'm willing to try. So, being honest for a change, here is a tale of warning with an end as vexing as the question of mortality itself.

Nobody has ever denied the gift of melodrama that rare birds bestow on us but sometimes their timing seems inspired by an almost demonic sense of wickedness. Exclusive their appearances may be, yet why must they also coincide with wedding anniversaries, christenings or, worst of all, the last shopping day before Christmas? In 1994, that was Saturday 24 December, about one o'clock in the afternoon.

"It certainly sounds like the real thing." I'm always wary of statements like that. This time I was forced to agree with my confrere's assessment. A farmer had discovered the bird that morning in his carrot fields. He said it was: "about the size of a donkey, had a rear end like a feather duster and was grey with a black and white head." He also wanted to know if it was likely to eat free-range hens.

My mind was racing. A Crane in Northern Ireland – unbelievable. At most, there were just two hours of daylight left and the bird was about an hour's drive away. What should I do? 'I can do all things through Christ which strengthen me. Philippians 4:13.' Okay, I'd go for it.

I commandeered the family car, collected a scrambled posse en route, and set off like a boy racer. First problem: Christmas shopping traffic. I detoured at rallye speed onto uncongested country roads, watching – in my case – the ominously low glimmer of the setting sun or, in the case of my passengers, the state of the ungritted roads we were zooming along and the occasional sparkle of ice. I thought they looked a bit shifty. "Sorry lads, on these roads 70mph is about as fast as I can manage." For some reason they continued to look impassive, stiff even.

Pausing just once, to check the map at the crossroads, the Exocet-like pace kept darkness and other road users at bay right up to the moment when we arrived at the desired network of fields. Overhead the clouds were dark and strange. I was about to voice my concern that the Crane might have already gone

In the middle of life's humdrum you can be pitched onto a journey whose destination nobody knows.

195

to roost, when it happened. Someone yelled, "STOP, I SEE IT!" I hit the brakes; the car slid, spun, skidded involuntarily and ploughed straight into a low wall. I ricocheted off the steering wheel and caught a wiper blade full in the mouth as I impacted through the windscreen. No seat belt, no chance. I will never forget the pain. The crushing, searing sensation in my chest and – my head – bludgeoned and numb, now engulfed by a horrible darkness. I could not see. My senses had been replaced with a void. Silence.

Then, still trapped in the driving seat, something quite astonishing happened. My eyes slowly adjusted to the gloom and I started to discern the road, the frosted fields and the car. Its front was crumpled and shrouded in steam from a fractured radiator. From an elevated perspective I saw my companions emerge, shaken but mercifully unhurt. I could hear their voices. They tore at my door and shouted at me, "Come on, the Crane's still here," and then saw my ghastly face and twisted torso. I was unrecognizable to myself. Where was I?

Extempore celestial thoughts entered my head. Of a life ebbing and oblivion beckoning. But wait. The Crane. I could see it! I hadn't noticed it until it raised its head. Fantastic – and so close to the road. No wonder we'd almost driven past it. Even better, the lads were watching it too. YEAH! I tried to communicate with them. Perchance to scratch with a bloodied finger the words "Got it" in the roadside mud, but it was no use.

Out of nowhere a wind sprang up as if to prevent me looking down any longer. My mind became clouded and confused. Above, a dim tracery of stars in the firmament seemed to draw me towards them. I felt weightless, not of this world, as though all my bodily atoms had departed. I sensed an overwhelming urge to stop this process. Clouds enveloped me and then I heard ceremonial organ music. A choir sang, "Lo! What a glorious sight appears to our admiring eyes, the former seas have passed away, the former earth and skies."

At this, a chilling panic gripped me. With a last Herculean effort I gasped, "Hell no – I won't go. ICH BIN EIN BIRDER!"

Others told me what happened next. The ride in the ambulance, the dash to the emergency room, unconsciousness as the medical team fought to save my life and the long bedside vigils of friends and family while I languished in a coma. I have since recovered, my faculties intact, but still the dilemma remains – can I count the Crane?

April 1995
Birdwatch

Photographic index

Except where noted, all photographs taken by Anthony McGeehan. Page numbers given.

No more Mr Nice Guy
53   Blackcap (Eurasian Blackcap) *Sylvia atricapilla*, Bangor, Down, Northern Ireland, February 2009

Shore wars
54   Common Sandpiper *Actitis hypoleucos*, Belfast, Antrim, Northern Ireland, August 2007

Enlightenment, not epitaphs
59   Rifle stock and telescope, New Jersey, USA, May 1993

Faith, hope and ternery
63   Arctic Tern *Sterna paradisaea*, Groomsport, Down, Northern Ireland, June 2006
64   Helicopter over tern nesting island, Harbour Lagoon, Belfast Harbour Estate, Antrim, Northern Ireland, April 2005 (*Tom Ennis*)

Reign in Spain
69   From top left:
       Audouin's Gull *Larus audouinii*,
       Scopoli's Shearwater *Calonectris diomedea*,
       Pomarine Skua *Stercorarius pomarinus*,
       European Bee-eater *Merops apiaster* (*Tom Ennis*),
       Zitting Cisticola *Cisticola juncidis*,
       Melodious Warbler *Hippolais polyglotta*,
       Black Wheatear *Oenanthe leucura* (*Tom Ennis*),
       Short-toed Lark (Greater Short-toed Lark) *Calandrella brachydactyla*,
       Collared Pratincole *Glareola pratincola*,
       Greater Flamingos *Phoenicopterus roseus*,
       Black-winged Stilt *Himantopus himantopus*

Sun, sea ... and him
73   Audouin's Gull *Larus audouinii*, Mallorca, Balearic Islands, Spain, April 1993

Douze Pointes Lark
74   Magnus Robb, Belchite, Zaragoza, Spain, February 2008
77   Dupont's Lark *Chersophilus duponti*, Tizi-n-Taghatine, Morocco, January 2004 (*Ran Schols*)
78   Belchite, Zaragoza, Spain, February 2008

Letter from America
80   Bruce Mactavish, High Point State Park, Sussex, New Jersey, USA, May 1997
83   Hermit Thrush *Catharus guttatus*, Alberta, Canada, 6 October 2005 (*Gerald Romanchuk*)

The big one
84   Bald Eagle *Haliaeetus leucocephalus*, Homer, Alaska, USA, 20 June 2004 (*René Pop*)

Mental in Manitoba
88   Hawk Owl (Northern Hawk-Owl) *Surnia ulula*, Alberta, Canada, October 2005 (*Gerald Romanchuk*)

CD contents

CD1-01   Boy meets rail
narrated by Anthony McGeehan

music excerpts from **A Parliament of Rooks**, performed by The Village Band, written by Simon Emmerson, Kate Garrett and Barney Morse Brown, published by Real World Music and Garrett/Brown Music

excerpts from bird recordings
0:50-1:21   **Corncrake (Corn Crake)** *Crex crex* Inishbofin, Donegal, Ireland, 04:27, 13 June 2008. Song of male, with other males further away.
7:56-8:25   Background: Meadow Pipit *Anthus pratensis*, Winter Wren *Troglodytes troglodytes*. 080613.MR.042739.21

6:32-6:33   **Corncrake (Corn Crake)** *Crex crex* Midwolda, Groningen, Netherlands, 02:54, 24 July 2003. Wingbeats of a male when flushed. 03.028.AB.13655.00

CD1-02   Great Northern Diva
narrated by Anthony McGeehan

music excerpt from **Great Northern Diva Theme**, performed and written by Simon Emmerson and Richard Evans, published by Real World Music and **Tales of the Riverbank**, narrated by Johnny Morris, reproduced by kind permission of Granada International

excerpts from bird recordings
2:47-3:58   **Sedge Warbler** *Acrocephalus schoenobaenus* Oostelijke Binnenpolder, Noord-Holland, Netherlands, 03:34, 5 June 2006. Song of a
5:50-6:45   male. 060605.MR.33413.00

2:47-3:58   **Lapwing (Northern Lapwing)** *Vanellus vanellus* Wareham, Dorset, England, 20:00, 20 April 2007. Alarms possibly due to a fox.
5:50-6:45   Background: female Common Shelduck *Tadorna tadorna*, displaying Common Snipe *Gallinago gallinago* and Eurasian Curlew *Numenius arquata*. 07.005.MC.03555.01

2:52-3:58   **Tawny Owl** *Strix aluco* Abernethy Forest, Highland, Scotland, 19 March 2002. Song of a male. 02.010.MR.01437.10
5:50-6:45

6:24-7:32   **Great Northern Diver (Great Northern Loon)** *Gavia immer* Mývatn, Iceland, 01:00, 24 June 2003. Wails of a paired adult. Background: wingbeats and calls of female Red-breasted Merganser *Mergus serrator*, Common Snipe *Gallinago gallinago*, Arctic Tern *Sterna paradisaea* and Redwing *Turdus iliacus*. 03.031.MR.03946.01

CD1-03   Gallocanta
narrated by Anthony McGeehan

music excerpts from **The Gallocanta Theme** and **First Rain**, both performed and written by Simon Emmerson and Richard Evans, published by Real World Music

excerpts from bird recordings
10:43-11:58   **Crane (Common Crane)** *Grus grus* Gallocanto lake, Aragón, Spain, 6 February 2008. A huge flock of more than 500 flying low over the recordist who was cowering in a ditch. Whistling calls of juveniles can be heard from time to time. Background: Common Linnets *Carduelis cannabina* and Corn Bunting *Emberiza calandra*. 080206.MR.115200.01

CD1-04 Who dares wins **narrated by Anthony McGeehan**
music excerpt from ***Surfin' Bird***, performed by The Trashmen, written by Alfred Frazier, Carl White, Turner Wilson and John Harris, published by Ardmore And Beechwood Ltd

CD1-05 My life with a jerk **narrated by Mairead McGeehan**
excerpts from bird recordings

2:29-2:39   **Snow Finch (White-winged Snowfinch)** *Montifringilla nivalis* Demirkazık, Adana, Turkey, 5 May 2001. Calls of an adult taking off. 01.016.MR.03645.00

2:50-2:58   **Alpine Accentor** *Prunella collaris* Montserrat, Catalunya, Spain, 14:05, 8 February 2008. Loud calls on taking off from a feeding station. 080208.MR.140549.01

3:46-3:55   **Ring-billed Gull** *Larus delawarensis* Titusville, Brevard, Florida, USA, 10:29, 5 February 2005. Long call of an adult, presumed male. 05.001.AB.04039.11

6:19-6:48   **Ringed Plover (Common Ringed Plover)** *Charadrius hiaticula* Texel, Noord-Holland, Netherlands, 11:00, 17 February 2005. Display flight of a male joined by a second bird, possibly a female. Background: Eurasian Oystercatcher *Haematopus ostralegus* and Snow Bunting *Plectrophenax nivalis*. 05.001.MR.01341.01

CD1-06 Kids' stuff **narrated by Anthony McGeehan**
music excerpt from ***Cross the Wetlands***, performed by The Imagined Village, written by Martin Carthy, Simon Emmerson and Richard Evans, published by Real World Music and Topic Music

CD1-07 Bless me Father **narrated by Anthony McGeehan**
excerpts from bird recordings

6:28-6:39   **Long-billed Dowitcher** *Limnodromus scolopaceus* Prudhoe Bay, Alaska, USA, 01:24, 15 June 2004. Flight calls of an adult before, during and after take-off. 04.018.AB.13422.11

CD1-08 Shore wars **narrated by Anthony McGeehan**
excerpts from bird recordings

3:06-3:18   **Redshank (Common Redshank)** *Tringa totanus* Breskens, Zeeland, Netherlands, 09:00, 23 April 2006. Calls of a migrating individual are answered from an occupied territory below. 06.006.MR.15053.21

3:06-3:18   **Turnstone (Ruddy Turnstone)** *Arenaria interpres* Griend, Friesland, Netherlands, 11 September 2005. A small flock of adults and juveniles takes off. 05.025.MR.11448.11

3:15-3:47   **Bar-tailed Godwit** *Limosa lapponica* Griend, Friesland, Netherlands, 12:57, 15 April 2006. A huge flock takes off as high tide approaches. 06.005.MR.10510.00

CD1-09 Sun, sea and … him
narrated by Mairead McGeehan

music excerpt from **The Blackbird**, performed by Rachael Unthank and The Winterset, written by Belinda O'Hooley, published by Copyright Control

excerpts from bird recordings

0:55-1:31   **Albufera marsh**, Mallorca, Balearic Islands, Spain, 28 May 2003. Ambient recording with Common Moorhen *Gallinula chloropus*, Western Swamphen *Porphyrio porphyrio*, Eurasian Coot *Fulica atra*, Zitting Cisticola *Cisticola juncidis*, Moustached Warbler *Acrocephalus melanopogon*, Great Reed Warbler *A arundinaceus*. 03.018.MC.00440.10

2:05-2:33   **Hoopoe (Eurasian Hoopoe)** *Upupa epops* Sierra de Gredos, Extremadura, Spain, 07:35, 12 June 2002. Song. Background: Common Chaffinch *Fringilla coelebs*. 02.018.AB.13521.01

2:08-2:15   **Osprey** *Pandion haliaetus* Raso, Cape Verde Islands, 13:13, 21 March 2007. Chirping calls of a pair. 070321.MR.131303.00

2:14-2:25   **Audouin's Gull** *Larus audouinii* Port de Pollenca, Mallorca, Balearic Islands, Spain, 15:00, 12 April 2002. Long call of an adult on a small breakwater along the beach. 02.009.MC.10400.01

6:05-6:17   **Pallid Swift** *Apus pallidus* Petra, Jordan, 4 May 2004. Calls by individuals flying in and out of breeding cave. Background: House Sparrows *Passer domesticus*. 04.016.MR.03620.00

CD2-01 Letter from America
narrated by Anthony McGeehan

music excerpts from **A Parliament of Rooks**, performed by The Village Band, written by Simon Emmerson, Kate Garrett and Barney Morse Brown, published by Real World Music and Garrett/Brown Music

excerpts from bird recordings

7:41-7:51   **Sora** *Porzana carolina* Frank Lake, Alberta, Canada, 09:06, 9 June 2003. Descending 'whinny' characteristic of this species. Background: Savannah Sparrow *Passerculus sandwichensis*, Yellow-headed Blackbird *Xanthocephalus xanthocephalus*. 03.024.AB.12040.00

7:54-7:58   **Blackpoll Warbler** *Dendroica striata* Nome, Alaska, USA, 13:24, 1 June 2004. Song of a male. 04.012.AB.04630.00

8:01-8:03   **Bobolink** *Dolichonyx oryzivorus* Cape May, New Jersey, USA, 26 September 2004. Single call of a migrant flying through the night. 04.009.KM.03756.11

9:05-10:50   **Hermit Thrush** *Catharus guttatus* High Point, New Jersey, USA, 11 May 1994. Song of a male during a thunder storm. Mark Constantine.

CD2-02 Warden's report
narrated by Mairead McGeehan

music excerpt from **Summer's End**, performed by Jackie Oates, written by Jim Causley, published by Copyright Control

CD2-03 Heir line
narrated by Anthony McGeehan

excerpts from bird recordings

5:47-6:03   **Ortolan Bunting** *Emberiza hortulana* IJmuiden, Noord-Holland, Netherlands, 17 September 2003. Several calls of a first-winter male taking off and flying a short distance. Background: Meadow Pipit *Anthus pratensis*, Eurasian Magpie *Pica pica* and Eurasian Siskin *Carduelis spinus*. 03.035.MR.12128.00

5:57-6:24 **Lapland Bunting (Lapland Longspur)** *Calcarius lapponicus* IJmuiden, Noord-Holland, Netherlands, 28 September 2002. Rattle and *tew* calls of an autumn migrant. Meadow Pipit *Anthus pratensis*. 02.043.MR.03015.21

CD2-04   Time to take him away   narrated by Mairead McGeehan
music excerpt from **Take Him Away Theme**, performed and written by Simon Emmerson, published by Real World Music

CD2-05   Gyr crazy   narrated by Anthony McGeehan
music excerpt from **It's Only a Raven**, performed and written by Simon Emmerson and Richard Evans, published by Real World Music

excerpts from bird recordings
1:41-2:20 **Gyr (Gyrfalcon)** *Falco rusticolus* Mývatn, Iceland, 23 June 2003. Calls and wingbeats of an adult female. Background: Redwing *Turdus iliacus*. 03.031.MR.03000.20

CD2-06   A trip to Iceland   narrated by Anthony McGeehan
music excerpts from **Burton Beach**, performed and written by The Village Band, published by Real World Music, **Lapwings at Night**, written by Simon Emmerson and Richard Evans, published by Real World Music and **Lark in the Morning**, traditional, performed and arranged by Jackie Oates, published by Copyright Control

excerpts from bird recordings
4:08-5:13 **Song Thrush** *Turdus philomelos* Roe Valley Country Park, Derry, Northern Ireland, 19 March 2008. Intense, 'ultra-crystallised' song of two males at dusk. 080319.MR.191227.21

7:09-7:48 **Dipper (White-throated Dipper)** *Cinclus cinclus* Crawfordsburn, Down, Northern Ireland, 20 March 2008. Song. 080320. MR.104159.23

15:26-18:12 **Lapwing (Northern Lapwing)** *Vanellus vanellus* Tory Island, Donegal, Ireland, 23:59, 18 March 2008. Males displaying at night. Background: Eurasian Oystercatcher *Haematopus ostralegus*, Common Snipe *Gallinago gallinago* and Common Redshank *Tringa totanus*. 080318.MR.235945.00

15:31-18:33 **Lapwing (Northern Lapwing)** *Vanellus vanellus* Tory Island, Donegal, Ireland, 21:06, 17 March 2008. Males displaying at night. Background: Eurasian Oystercatcher *Haematopus ostralegus* and Common Redshank *Tringa totanus*. 080317.MR.210644.00

18:00-22:35 **Skylark (Eurasian Skylark)** *Alauda arvensis* Tory Island, Donegal, Ireland, 09:13, 19 March 2008. Overlapping songflights of three males, each one closer than the preceding. Background: Great Northern Loon *Gavia immer*, Northern Lapwing *Vanellus vanellus* and Meadow Pipit *Anthus pratensis*. 080319.MR.091357.01

CD2-07
Gulls n' roses   narrated by Mairead McGeehan
excerpts from bird recordings
1:42-2:48 **Iceland Gull** *Larus glaucoides* Thorlakshofn (Þorlákshöfn) fishing harbour, Iceland, 17 March 2003. A feeding flock of individuals of all ages, possibly including one or two calls of a Glaucous Gull *Larus hyperboreus*. 03.006.MR.02600.02

Books published by The Sound Approach

The Sound Approach to Birding: a guide to understanding bird sound
by Mark Constantine & The Sound Approach 2006

... bringing us the most important advance birding has seen over the last decade. ... deservedly wins the column's annual award for the best bird book. (Stuart Winter, Sunday Express December 2006.)

Birdwatch Bird Book of the Year 2006 and winner of the British Birds & British Trust for Ornithology Award for Best Bird Book of the Year 2006.

The Sound Approach to birding has a relaxed, humorous and easy-to-read style, combining scientific theory, practical field experience and anecdote. All birders who 'don't do calls' or who take fright at the first glimpse of a sonagram would be well advised to read it. They should find it a revelation. (John Brucker, Ibis 149(4) 2007.)

... like a new religion. ... There is no question that every serious birder should have this book. (Keith Betton, Birding World 20(3): 131, 2006.)

Petrels night and day: a Sound Approach guide
by Magnus Robb, Killian Mullarney & The Sound Approach 2008

Unique subject matter that informs and entertains. A writing style that captivates readers and holds their interest. Production values that exceed expectations, presenting material in an original and refreshing format. Images that bring the subject matter to life. If all these boxes – and more – have been ticked, then you know you are onto a winner. ... A truly unique work and a deserving winner of the title Birdwatch Bird Book of the Year 2008 (Birdwatch 201: 54, March 2009.)

Petrels night and day carries high the banner of the pioneering birding spirit, and lives up to all of the audacious thoughts and actions of its first-born sister volume. ... marvel at the sounds and sights of, comfortably, the best bird book of 2008. (Mark Golley, www.birdguides.com September 2008.)